CW00734694

Collins *Little book of*

# SCRABBLE™
BRAND Crossword Game
# SECRETS

*Mark Nyman*

**HarperCollins Publishers**
Westerhill Road
Bishopbriggs
Glasgow
G64 2QT

Second edition 2016

10 9 8 7 6 5 4 3 2 1

© HarperCollins Publishers 2011, 2014, 2016

ISBN 978-0-00-758915-9

www.collinsdictionary.com
www.harpercollins.co.uk/scrabble

A catalogue record for this book is available
from the British Library

Typeset by Davidson Publishing Solutions,
Glasgow

Printed and bound by RR Donnelley APS

A catalogue record for this book is available
from the British Library

If you would like to comment on any aspect
of this book, please contact us at the above
address or online.
E-mail: puzzles@harpercollins.co.uk
 facebook.com/collinsdictionary
 @collinsdict

**Written by:** Mark Nyman

**Editors:** Freddy Chick, Barry Grossman

**For the Publisher:** Gerry Breslin, Kerry Ferguson

# Foreword

Mark Nyman is pretty cool, off and on the Scrabble board. He takes the game seriously but also gets a lot of fun out of it.

I was in the audience when Mark won the 1993 World Championships. As a sports enthusiast, I've been to a few sporting events – Wimbledon Finals, World Cup Cricket, etc – and I can honestly say that I've never experienced an atmosphere like that. Trailing 2 games to 1 in a best of 5 final to the Canadian Joel Wapnick, Mark recovered from a 180 point deficit in the fourth game to win that game, going on to take the title. Yes, people were standing on their seats and cheering over a game of Scrabble!

I was also at the 1999 World Final where he lost the deciding game to the same opponent by just one point.

Uniquely amongst the world's best players, Mark has experienced the highs and lows of Scrabble at its ultimate level, but he has retained his passion and joy for the game. This comes across, in spades, in this short but comprehensive book, aimed at beginners but with something for players of all abilities – even if it's just the 'skulduggery' section, which is a must-read!

This second edition has been revised so that it is in line with the latest publication of the authorized Scrabble wordlist – *Collins Official Scrabble Words*.

*Philip Nelkon*
4-time National Scrabble Champion

# Essential Scrabble Glossary

**Blockers** are words which cannot have a letter added to either the beginning or the end. This means blockers often 'close down' part of the board.

**Bonuses** are words, usually seven or eight letters long, which use all of your tiles to give you an extra 50 points.

**Floaters** are letters that are available on the board for you to use as part of another word, and to play onto.

**Hooks** are words than can be transformed into another valid word by the addition of a single letter at the beginning or the end. For example:

**EARFUL** can take a **T** at the front to make **TEARFUL**

**SEA** can take a **T** at the end to make **SEAT**

# 1 | Two's Company

Scrabble study always starts with the 2-letter words. The most useful of these are the ones with the highest-scoring letters, i.e. the **Q** and **Z**. So let's begin with the three most useful words in Scrabble:

**QI**        Life force

**ZA**        Pizza

**ZO**        Himalayan cattle

So if an **I**, **A** or **O** is directly below or to the right of a triple letter square, you could place the **Q** or **Z** on it and, if you can go across/down with the same word, a potential 62 points can be picked up, much to the consternation of your opponent!

## 2 | Less Is More

A common myth amongst Scrabble beginners is that the longer the word, the higher the score – this is not necessarily true at all.

You may **AGONIZE** for as little as 17 if you don't make good use of the premium squares, whereas as in secret 1 a simple **ZO** or **ZA** might get you 62 on the same turn – be economical with your tiles.

## 3  Starters

**S**, **C** and **P** respectively are the most common starting letters and together comprise over a quarter of the words in the dictionary. So when moving your rack around it's a good idea to put them at the beginning – a profusion of words arise from such useful prefixes as:

**SEMI-, SUB-**

**CH-, CO-**

**POLY-, PRE-**

# 4 | Meaning-less?

Whether or not to insist on knowing the meanings of words played is a controversial topic and can lead to lots of arguments.

The official rule is that you don't have to know them, but some people still think it's just not right. If you are playing at home and insist on knowing the meanings it can lead to trouble because it's a moot point how close you have to get to the exact definition. For example, you may play **ZLOTY** knowing it's a type of currency, but your opponent may insist on you explaining from which country it originates. If you don't know, will they let you have the word?

These inconsistencies can cause a fallout, so far better to stick to the 'not having to know' rule for peace's sake. It's great to find out the meanings, but when there are 157,000 Scrabble words with 9 letters or less, it would take an incredible mind to know every meaning as well as every word.

Personally, I would rather learn a new word than a meaning of an existing word I know (shock horror), but I do enjoy picking up some of the meanings along the way. Former World Champion Pakorn Nemitrmansuk from Thailand struggles with fluent English and doesn't bother with the meanings of the more outlandish words.

On the other hand, Scrabble is a great learning tool for improving vocabulary, so at the end of the day it's whatever floats your boat. Just don't sneer at your opponent if they don't know a definition unless you think they'd do the same to you.

## 5 | Pardon Me

The 6-letter combination **PARDON** goes with every vowel to make an unusual 7-letter word and thereby give a possible 50-point bonus:

**PARDON** + **A** PANDORA – sea bream
           + **E** PADRONE – Italian inn owner
           + **I** PONIARD – dagger
           + **O** PANDOOR – a force of brutal
                     Croatian soldiers
           + **U** PANDOUR – "    "    "    "

By the way **PARDON ME** is an anagram of **POMANDER**.

## 6 | No Rush

Use all of your 25 minutes when you play to a clock. Don't rush into playing the first move you think of – there's usually a better move you haven't spotted yet.

It's also worth giving yourself a couple of extra seconds after placing your move on the board and before hitting the clock to make sure you're happy with it.

# Hello
# Hello
# Hello

There are no less than thirteen different variations of the word **HELLO**:

| | |
|---|---|
| **HALLO** | **HOLLO** |
| **HALLALOO** | **HOLLOA** |
| **HALLOA** | **HOLLOO** |
| **HALLOO** | **HULLO** |
| **HILLO** | **HULLOA** |
| **HILLOA** | **HULLOO** |
| **HOLLA** | |

They are all verbs (apart from **HALLALOO**) and **HALLOES**, **HELLOES**, **HILLOES**, **HOLLOES** and **HULLOES** are also okay, so there are forty-five derivatives altogether.

# Irritable Vowel Syndrome

Too many vowels on your rack can lead to disaster. Generally, the ideal ratio of consonants to vowels is 4:3. So having four vowels is a slight overload but fairly easily remedied – five or more and the alarm bells start ringing.

In this case, it can take two or three turns to restore the balance, and the worst of it is you are unlikely to score well in the meantime since the vowels are worth only one point at face value.

Here are some examples of lovely **vowelly** words to get you out of trouble quickly:

| | |
|---|---|
| **AE** | one |
| **AI** | slow moving shaggy South American animal |
| **EA** | a river |
| **IO** | moth |
| **OI** | shout for attention |
| **OU** | man |
| **AIA** | Eastern female servant |
| **AUA** | mullet |
| **AUE** | Maori exclamation |
| **EAU** | a river |
| **EUOI** | a cry of Bacchic frenzy |
| **EUOUAE** | a Gregorian cadence |

It's amazing how often **EUOI** especially comes up – those followers of Bacchus had some fun didn't they?

## 9 | A Fine Mess

You can easily get out of a sticky situation with multiple **A**s if you know some of these:

| | |
|---|---|
| **AA** | volcanic lava |
| **AAL** | Asian tree |
| **ABA** | Syrian camel-haired cloth |
| **AKA** | New Zealand vine |
| **ALA** | wing |
| **AMA** | water vessel |
| **ANA** | collection of reminiscences |
| **AVA** | Polynesian shrub |
| **AWA** | away |
| **CAA** | to call |
| **FAA** | fall |
| **MAA** | to bleat |
| **ACAI** | Brazilian berry |
| **ANOA** | small cattle |
| **ATUA** | demon |
| **AULA** | hall |
| **ABACA** | Philippine plant |
| **ALAAP** | Indian rhythm |
| **ALAPA** | "          " |
| **ANANA** | pineapple |
| **ARABA** | Asian carriage |
| **TAATA** | father |
| **ARAARA** | game fish |
| **TAIAHA** | Maori staff |

## 10 | E by Gum

**E** is the most common letter and the best vowel to hold. You can really struggle with a dearth of **E**s in the game – they are its lifeblood – but on the flip side, you don't really want more than a couple on your rack at any one time. Because there are twelve in the set, you can quite often find yourself with three or four **E**s – here are a few words to **E**s the problem:

| | |
|---|---|
| **EE** | eye |
| **EEN** | eyes |
| **EME** | uncle |
| **ENE** | even |
| **JEE** | to move ahead |
| **MEE** | Malaysian noodle dish |
| **EEVEN** | evening |
| **ELPEE** | long-playing record |
| **ETWEE** | small case |
| **EXEME** | to set free |
| **GELEE** | jelly |
| **ENTETE** | obsessed |
| **VEEPEE** | vice president |
| **VENEWE** | venue |

Do however try and keep one **E** back on your rack unless the score with it is too good to miss.

# 11 | For Your Is Only

It's amazing how regularly you can get stuck with two or three Is on your rack and, if you're not careful, the problem can persist. To dig you out of the I-hole sooner rather than later, try playing the following:

| | | | |
|---|---|---|---|
| **IWI** | Maori tribe | **WILI** | spirit |
| **BIDI** | Indian cigarette | **AALII** | bushy shrub |
| **DIVI** | stupid person | **BIKIE** | motorcycle gang member |
| **FINI** | finish | | |
| **HILI** | scar on a seed | **CIVIE** | civilian |
| **IMID** | a drug | **DIXIE** | cooking pot |
| **INIA** | points at the back of the head | **FIXIT** | solution to a problem |
| | | **LITAI** | Lithuanian monetary unit |
| **IRID** | iris | | |
| **IXIA** | African plant | **MIRIN** | Japanese rice wine |
| **LIRI** | monetary unit | | |
| **NIDI** | insects' nests | **OIDIA** | fungal spores |
| **PILI** | Philippine tree | **TEIID** | lizard |
| **TITI** | South American monkey | **VISIE** | to look |
| | | **YITIE** | bunting |
| | | **ZIMBI** | cowrie shell |

## 12 | O My Word

A surfeit of **O**s is relatively easy to alleviate, but here's a soupçon of gems to make it even simpler:

| | |
|---|---|
| **OO** | wool |
| **OBO** | ship carrying oil |
| **ONO** | Hawaiian fish |
| **OOM** | old man's title of respect |
| **OOR** | our |
| **OOT** | out |
| **OXO** | acid containing oxygen |
| **OLIO** | dish of differing ingredients |
| **ORZO** | pasta |
| **OVOLO** | convex moulding |
| **GOOROO** | guru |
| **HOOROO** | hurrah |

# 13 | U-seless

The **U** is by far the least useful of the vowels, unless of course accompanied by the **Q**. More than one **U** can really cramp your style and flow, but there are a few unusual multiple **U**-words that can help:

| | |
|---|---|
| **ULU** | knife |
| **UMU** | oven |
| **UTU** | reward |
| **BUBU** | African garment |
| **HUHU** | hairy New Zealand beetle |
| **KURU** | nervous disease |
| **LULU** | outstanding person |
| **PUPU** | Hawaiian dish |
| **RURU** | owl |
| **SULU** | Fijian sarong |
| **UNAU** | two-toed sloth |
| **URUS** | extinct European ox |
| **YUZU** | citrus fruit |
| **AHURU** | Pacific cod |
| **BUTUT** | Gambian monetary unit |
| **DURUM** | Mediterranean wheat |
| **QUIPU** | Incan recording device |
| **UHURU** | national independence |
| **URUBU** | bird |
| **MUUMUU** | Hawaiian dress |

# 14 Vocabulary

A player's vocabulary is their ammunition in the game. It's not the 'be all and end all' but the more words you know, the more you should improve. An average person's vocabulary is between 10–15,000 words, i.e. about 10% of all the words useful to Scrabble, so there's plenty of scope for improvement.

Don't be put off at the thought of having to learn 100,000 new words. If you're willing to give it a go, you can be economical with your study as some words are a lot more 'Scrabble-friendly' than others. The best players probably know about half of them and there are only a handful of people close to knowing the lot – and they definitely need to get out more...

## 15 | Size Matters

The 2-letter words are the bread and butter of Scrabble, and learning them is by no means an insurmountable task. There are just 124 twos of which about a third are everyday words anyway, so learning two or three a day will crack them all in the space of a month.

Next come the 1341 3-letter words. Only the top players know all these, but it's surprising how many you will pick up with practice.

The more weird and wonderful 4s and 5s are reserved for the serious player – if you're starting out on the competitive road, it's best to kick off by learning those with the high-scoring letters.

The 6s aren't as important as you might think and probably come last in a study regime. However, there are some fabulous 6-letter blockers worth knowing.

The high-probability 7s and 8s are really useful in the search for that treasured 50-point bonus. There are about 34,000 7-letter words in all and 42,000 eights, but don't let that deter you. Knowledge of the most likely 250 of each will improve your game immensely.

9-letter (or longer) words come up very rarely, though it's incredibly satisfying when they do. In terms of Scrabble study don't worry about them – that saves you looking at half the dictionary.

## 16 | Some Real Corkers

Here's an **A** to **Z** of some of my favourite 7s and 8s:

| | |
|---|---|
| **AZULEJO** | Spanish porcelain tile |
| **BUHUNDS** | Norwegian dogs |
| **CONEPATL** | skunk |
| **DWEEBISH** | quite stupid |
| **EUPHRASY** | annual plant |
| **FIREFANG** | to overheat through decomposition |
| **GUNKHOLE** | to go on short boat excursions |
| **HEITIKI** | Maori neck ornament |
| **ICEKHANA** | motor race on frozen lake |
| **JEREPIGO** | fortified wine |
| **KERCHOO** | atishoo |
| **LUNKHEAD** | stupid person |
| **MRIDANGA** | Indian drum |
| **NUDZHES** | nudges |
| **OLYCOOK** | American doughnut |
| **PATOOTIE** | person's bottom |
| **QUETZAL** | Central American bird |
| **RUDESBY** | rude person |
| **SLYBOOTS** | sly person |
| **TAGHAIRM** | divination sought by lying in a bullock's hide under a Scottish waterfall |

| | |
|---|---|
| **UNSHRUBD** | not having shrubs |
| **VEEJAYS** | video jockeys |
| **WOSBIRD** | illegitimate child |
| **XERAFIN** | Indian coin |
| **YAHOOISM** | crudeness |
| **ZEDOARY** | Asian stem used as a stimulant |

# 17 | Time for a Change

There is a great deal of skill in choosing the right time to change your letters, as well as which ones to throw back in the bag.

The first, and most important, tip on this subject is DON'T BE AFRAID TO CHANGE. You may score zero on that particular turn, but if the alternative is to be left with a horrible combination of letters, like **IIIUVVW**, you may get stuck scoring ten points per move for several turns. Say you average twenty points per turn, it's better to change and score a likely sixty over the next three moves than forty without the change.

# 18 | Hold on to Your **Retsina**

The most 50-point bonus-conducive letters are **AEINRST** – generally, when throwing tiles in the bag, you want to keep one of any of these that you hold on your rack, as long as you leave a decent consonant to vowel ratio (i.e. 3:2, 2:2, 2:1, 1:1). The highest scoring letters **JQXZ** are only worth keeping if there are some tasty triple-letter and triple-word squares available to play onto the board. If the board is tight and especially if there are no floating vowels, the high-scorers could be rendered useless. The **X** and **Z** are generally more fruitful than the **J** and **Q** if you can't resist holding one back.

## 19 | Chuck 'Em In

In my opinion, the converse of **AEINRST** is **FGJQUVW** – i.e. these are the seven worst letters in the set. So, when changing, always get rid of these unless you have the **Q** with a **U**, a high-scoring place for the **J**, or a promising **-ING** combination. Even then you might be held back, especially if the board is tight.

You may be surprised about the inclusion of the **G**, but in my experience **G**s are generally bad news. If you're deciding to change, always throw back a **V** if you have one. **V** is the weakest letter of all, partly because it's the only one that doesn't form a 2-letter word. As for the rest – **BCDHKLMOPXYZ** – they all have their merits and it depends on the state of the board as to whether any of them are worth keeping. Usually chuck them though.

## 20 | To the Max

**MAX**- is a handy prefix and produces some lovely extensions:

| | |
|---|---|
| **MAXED** | reached full extent |
| **MAXI** | large racing yacht |
| **MAXICOAT** | long coat |
| **MAXILLA** | upper jawbone |
| **MAXIMIN** | highest of set of minimum values |
| **MAXIMITE** | explosive |
| **MAXIMUS** | method rung on twelve bells |
| **MAXING** | reaching full extent |
| **MAXIXE** | Brazilian dance |
| **MAXWELL** | unit of magnetic flux |

There's also **SUPERMAX** – relating to the very highest levels of security.

Here's a selection of words to a-stone-ish you:

| | |
|---|---|
| **ASTONE** | astonish |
| **BURSTONE** | hard rock |
| **CAMSTONE** | limestone |
| **EARSTONE** | calcium carbonate crystal in the ear |
| **HISTONE** | DNA protein |
| **ICESTONE** | cryolite |
| **LAPSTONE** | cobbler's device |
| **POTSTONE** | used for making cooking vessels |
| **ROESTONE** | limestone |
| **RUBSTONE** | used for sharpening |
| **STONERAG** | lichen |
| **STONERAW** | lichen |
| **SUNSTONE** | feldspar |
| **TINSTONE** | black or brown stone |

There's also the 9-letter **IRONSTONE**, which is a very nice anagram of **SEROTONIN**, and **LIMESTONE** and **MILESTONE** are both anagrams of **LEMONIEST**.

## 22 | Take the Rough with the Smooth

Certain mini-combinations of consonants work really well together and are worth holding on to in the search for a 50-point bonus. They often tend to comprise both 'hard' and 'soft' letters but it's best not to keep back all 'hard' letters together and likewise all 'soft'.

'Hard' consonants **BDFGJKPQTVX**

'Soft' consonants **HLMNRSWYZ**

I've left out **C** as it can be both 'soft' and 'hard' – this adaptability is why it's a particular favourite.

So..........

# 23 In-consonants

Consonant combinations particularly worth keeping back for potential bonus play:

**BL, BM, BR, CH, CK, CN, CL, CR, CT, DL, DN, DR, HP, KL, KN, KR, LP, MP, NT, PR, RT**

**BDR, BLR, BMR, CDR, CHN, CHR, CHT, CLR, CLT, CNR, CNT, CRT, DLR, DNR, DPR, DRT, GLN, GNR, HPR, HNP, HPT, KLN, KLR, KNR, KNT, LPR, LPT, NRT, PRT**

An **S** is always worth holding on to in addition to these combinations. You will see they all contain at least one 'hard' and one 'soft' letter.

# 24 | Not In-consonants

Consonant combinations to avoid (using 3-point or lower tiles):

**BG, BP, CG, DT, GP, GT, LN**

**BDT, BGP, BGT, BPT, DGT, DGP, GPT, LNR**

You will notice that all these contain either all 'soft' or all 'hard' letters. Of course, any combination with two of the same letter and you automatically look to offload the duplicate.

**Licence to Thrill**

It can be good anagram practice to look at car number plates and try to find the shortest word you can using all the letters within them. Add any extra letters you want but the less the better, for example:

| | |
|---|---|
| SKO5 CYJ | **JOCKEYS** (beats **JOYSTICK**) |
| NCL2 END | **INCLINED** (beats **DECLINING**) |
| OWO6 ETA | **TEAKWOOD** (beats **TAEKWONDO**) |

This can be great fun and very satisfying on a long car journey but don't forget to concentrate on the road as well. Of course, you won't be able to find a word with all the plates – if you see QXO7 GJZ, give up immediately and move on to the next car.

## 26 | Tasty Twosomes

There are some gorgeous 7- and 8-letter anagram pairs – here are some of my favourites:

| | |
|---|---|
| APPRIZE | ZAPPIER |
| BOGEYMAN | MONEYBAG |
| CRUMPETS | SPECTRUM |
| DOORBELL | BORDELLO |
| ELATION | TOENAIL |
| FLUSHING | LUNGFISH (freshwater fish) |
| GHETTOED | DOGTEETH (carved ornaments) |
| HOGMANAY | MAHOGANY |
| IFFIEST | FIFTIES |
| JITTERS | TRIJETS (jets with three engines) |
| KIDNAPS | SKIDPAN (slippery area) |
| LIMEADE | EMAILED |
| MOORHEN | HORMONE |
| NAPPIES | PINESAP (red herb) |
| OOMPAHS | SHAMPOO |
| PRESUME | SUPREME |
| QUERIES | ESQUIRE |
| RINGTONE | NITROGEN |
| SCREWTOP | CROWSTEP (set of steps to the top of a gable) |
| TAPEWORM | POMWATER (kind of apple) |
| UTOPIAN | OPUNTIA (cactus) |

| VIOLATED | DOVETAIL |
| WASPNEST | STEWPANS |
| XEROTIC | EXCITOR (nerve) |
| YACKERS | SCREAKY |
| ZINCITE | CITIZEN |

**XEROTIC** is not as kinky as it sounds – it relates to dryness of bodily tissues.

# 27 Americanisms

As a general rule, all US alternative spellings are allowed in Scrabble, so color, humor, neighbor etc are OK - like it or not. Also, almost every **-ISE** verb can be spelt with **-IZE**. It's interesting that Collins is recognised everywhere in the World as the English Scrabble 'bible', apart from the US and Canada, where they use Webster's. Since Collins incorporates all of Webster's and a lot more, you ironically need to unlearn loads of words to play in the States. This seems a reflection of the US 'we are the world' attitude, so don't bother playing serious Scrabble over there.

South America is a relatively unexplored continent dictionarywise - there's plenty of scope for future great words from that neck of the woods.

# 28 Monkey Business

Monkeys keep ape-earing in the official Scrabble wordlist:

BANDARI
CEBID
COAITA
DOUC
ENTELLUS
GRIVET
GUEREZA
HANUMAN
JOCKO
LANGUR
MANGABEY

MICO
OUAKARI
OUISTITI
SAGOUIN
SAIMIRI
SAJOU
TALAPOIN
TAMARIN
VERVET
WANDEROO
ZATI

The beautiful **CYNOMOLGI** has to be worth a mention, however unlikely it is to jump out at you.

# 29 Slanguage

Slang words are perfectly allowable in Scrabble when they become common English usage.
A lot of Australian slang appears, such as:

| | |
|---|---|
| **ALF** | an uncultivated Australian |
| **SIK** | excellent |
| **ACCA** | an academic |
| **ALKO** | alcoholic |
| **DACK** | to forcefully remove trousers |
| **DOCO** | documentary |
| **DORB** | stupid person |
| **DRAC** | unattractive woman |
| **GOOG** | egg |
| **KERO** | kerosene |
| **KYBO** | temporary camping lavatory |
| **MYXO** | myxomatosis |
| **NOAH** | shark |
| **UMPY** | umpire |
| **WARB** | insignificant person |
| **FIRIE** | firefighter |
| **NIXER** | spare-time job |
| **UMPIE** | umpire |

**SLANGUAGE** is a word in itself – a lovely front hook to 'language'.

# 30 Feathered Friends

There are plenty of exotic **-BIRD** words to fly by you:

| | |
|---|---|
| **AXEBIRD** | nightjar |
| **BOOBIRD** | person who boos |
| **COWBIRD** | American songbird |
| **FATBIRD** | nocturnal bird |
| **GAOLBIRD** | person confined to jail |
| **HANGBIRD** | bird that builds a hanging nest |
| **JAYBIRD** | jay |
| **KINGBIRD** | American flycatcher |
| **LYREBIRD** | Australian bird that spreads its tail into shape of a lyre |
| **MAYBIRD** | American songbird |
| **OVENBIRD** | small South American bird |
| **PUFFBIRD** | tropical American bird |
| **RICEBIRD** | bird frequenting rice fields |
| **SNOWBIRD** | cocaine addict |
| **WHIPBIRD** | whistling bird |
| **YARDBIRD** | inexperienced soldier |

# 31 Abbreviations and Acronyms

Abbreviations are not allowed in themselves unless they come into common conversation, in which case they become colloquialisms, for example **AD** for advertisement. The same applies to acronyms – there are a few crackers:

| | |
|---|---|
| **ASPRO** | associate professor |
| **BAMBI** | born-again middle-aged biker |
| **ELINT** | electronic intelligence |
| **FEDEX** | federal express |
| **JATO** | jet-assisted take-off |
| **MIPS** | million instructions per second |
| **NOX** | nitrogen oxide |
| **POMO** | post-modernism |
| **QUANGO** | quasi-autonomous non-governmental organisation |
| **RONZER** | someone from rest of New Zealand – not Auckland |
| **TASER** | Thomas A. Swift's electric rifle |
| **TWOCCING** | taking without owner's consent |
| **WAAC** | member of Women's Auxiliary Arms Corps |
| **WOOPIE** | well-off older person |
| **YABA** | yet another bloody acronym! |

## 32 | **The Blank**

The blank is without doubt the best tile in the Scrabble set. If you're lucky enough to get both during the course of the game it will increase your chances of winning hugely, but you need to make the most of them.

If you get a blank early on, try and save it until you can use it in a 50-point bonus word. Never waste it on a move scoring less than 30 points.

Some players get really stuck when a blank appears – it's not surprising when you consider there are effectively twenty-six combinations to think about. But try to envisage the blank as a particular letter on your rack – some are more likely to go well with your other six letters than others. Even so, moves with a blank tend to require a great deal more thought and it's understandable they take longer.

As a general rule, use the blank when your move scores over 20 points more than one without it. Otherwise, hold on for a big play later – it's worth the wait.

Two blanks together can be a real mind-blower as there are 676 potential combinations. Don't panic: the more you play, the more you'll get a feel for which letters you're looking for them to be.

# 33 Bonus Play

If you can play out all your letters for the 50-point bonus, you'll enhance your winning chances enormously. Achieving this once in a game is good, twice excellent and three or more times will almost guarantee you victory.

The art of bonus finding is innate to Scrabble success – much of it is to do with rack-balancing along with knowing some high-probability 7- and 8-letter words (i.e. those with the most common letters) to help find that killer move.

There are some great 6- and 7-letter combinations to work towards to give yourself the best opportunity of making it happen.

## 34 | Another **Retsina**

As well as having ten anagrams (you don't need to know them all), **RETSINA** goes with more letters to make an 8-letter word than any other – so look for these floaters on the board:

**A** **ARTESIAN** (well)

**B** **BANISTER**

**C** **CANISTER**

**D** **STRAINED**

**E** **TRAINEES**

**F** **FENITARS**
(European plants)

**G** **ANGRIEST**

**H** **HAIRNETS**

**I** **RAINIEST**

**J** **NARTJIES**
(tangerines)

**K** **NARKIEST**

**L** **ENTRAILS**

**M** **MINARETS**

**N** **TRANNIES**

**O** **NOTARIES**

**P** **PAINTERS**

**R** **TRAINERS**

**S** **STAINERS**

**T** **NITRATES**

**U** **URINATES**

**W** **TINWARES**
(objects made of
tin plate)

## 35 | Anties in your Panties

The 6-letter combination **ANTIES** goes with more letters to make a 7-letter word than any other:

A **ENTASIA** (convex curve)

B **BASINET** (medieval helmet)

C **CINEAST** (film enthusiast)

D **DETAINS**

E **ETESIAN** (Mediterranean wind)

F **FAINEST** (most eager)

G **SEATING**

H **SHEITAN** (Muslim demon)

I **ISATINE** (yellowish-red compound)

J **JANTIES** (petty officers)

K **INTAKES**

L **ENTAILS**

M **INMATES**

N **INANEST**

O **ATONIES** (lack of muscle tone)

P **PANTIES**

R **RETSINA**

S **NASTIES**

T **INSTATE**

U **AUNTIES**

V **NATIVES**

W **TAWNIES**

X **SEXTAIN** (Italian verse)

Z **ZANIEST**

So only **Q** and **Y** don't work. Note that there are several anagrams in some cases but knowing one is often enough.

**Seating Room Only**

Along with **RETSINA**, **SEATING** is the most prolific 7-letter word when it comes to anagrams – it has ten:

**EASTING**    distance eastwards
**EATINGS**
**GAINEST**    straightest
**GENISTA**    member of broom family
**INGATES**    entrances
**INGESTA**    nourishment
**TAGINES**    African cooking pots
**TANGIES**    Orkney water spirits
**TEASING**
**TSIGANE**    Gypsy music

**-MAN** is a very productive suffix – here are some 7s and 8s you might not expect:

| | |
|---|---|
| **ADWOMAN** | woman working in advertising |
| **BRIDEMAN** | bridegroom's attendant |
| **CHOREMAN** | handyman |
| **DRAGOMAN** | Middle Eastern guide |
| **EARTHMAN** | inhabitant of the earth |
| **FACEMAN** | miner working at coalface |
| **GLEEMAN** | minstrel |
| **HELIMAN** | helicopter pilot |
| **IRONMAN** | very strong man |
| **JURYMAN** | member of a jury |
| **KEELMAN** | bargeman |
| **LOCOMAN** | railwayman |
| **MOTORMAN** | driver of electric train |
| **OVERSMAN** | overseer |
| **PRIZEMAN** | winner of prize |
| **QUILLMAN** | clerk |
| **RADIOMAN** | radio operator |
| **SWEETMAN** | Caribbean man kept by a woman |
| **TOYWOMAN** | woman who sells toys |
| **UNWOMAN** | to remove womanly qualities from |
| **VERSEMAN** | man who writes verse |
| **WATERMAN** | skilled boatman |
| **YEGGMAN** | burglar |

## 38 | De-stress

Part of the attraction of Scrabble is it helps you forget about your worries while you're concentrating on the game. Here are a few suggestions to make it an even more relaxing and positive experience:

(a) Sleep well the night before – a couple of beers or glasses of wine should do the trick
(b) Drink caffeine to stimulate your brain – not too much though as it might get a bit wayward
(c) Drink water – again in moderation as needing the loo will make you lose concentration
(d) Have a massage
(e) Play uplifting music
(f) Avoid stressful work and particularly bad bosses
(g) Avoid affairs
(h) Play in pleasant uncluttered surroundings
(i) Laugh at your opponent if they are over-competitive
(j) Support a winning football team, i.e. Barcelona or QPR

## 39 Wood You Believe It?

**WOOD** works really well as a prefix and suffix:

| | |
|---|---|
| **AGALWOOD** | Asian tree |
| **BEARWOOD** | bark used as a laxative |
| **CAMWOOD** | W. African tree |
| **DAGWOOD** | European shrub |
| **ELMWOOD** | wood from elm tree |
| **FATWOOD** | kindling |
| **GUMWOOD** | gumtree |
| **HAREWOOD** | sycamore |
| **INKWOOD** | tree |
| **KINGWOOD** | wood of Brazilian leguminous tree |
| **LATEWOOD** | formed later in tree's growing season |
| **MILKWOOD** | tree producing latex |
| **NUTWOOD** | walnut |
| **OVENWOOD** | word for burning in oven |
| **PEARWOOD** | wood from pear tree |
| **SAPWOOD** | soft wood beneath bark |
| **WILDWOOD** | forest growing in natural uncultivated state |
| **WOODBIN** | box for firewood |
| **WOODFREE** | paper from treated pulp |
| **WOODHEN** | flightless bird |
| **WOODLORE** | woodcraft skills |
| **WOODMEAL** | sawdust powder |
| **WOODMICE** | field mice |

| | |
|---|---|
| **WOODNESS** | quality of wood |
| **WOODNOTE** | natural musical note |
| **WOODROOF** | plant |
| **WOODSIA** | fern |
| **WOODSIER** | more connected with woods |
| **WOODSKIN** | canoe made of bark |
| **WOODTONE** | colour matching that of wood |
| **WOODWALE** | green woodpecker |
| **WOODWARD** | person in charge of wood |
| **WOODWOSE** | hairy wild man of the woods |

**Against All Odds**

**ANTI-** as a prefix gives rise to plenty of high-probability 7s and 8s – the meanings are mainly self-explanatory:

**ANTIACNE**
**ANTIBOSS**
**ANTICOLD**
**ANTIDORA** (bread used in Russian Orthodox Communion)
**ANTIFOG**
**ANTIGANG**
**ANTIJAM**
**ANTIKING** (a rival to an established king)
**ANTILEAK**
**ANTIMALE**
**ANTINUKE**
**ANTIPOT**
**ANTIROCK** (preventing a vehicle from rocking)
**ANTISNOB**
**ANTITAX**
**ANTIWEED**

## 41 Cheats Never Prosper

Cheating is a very tricky subject to cover. If you're just playing a casual game at home with a like-minded individual, cheating can be fun. However, if there is any degree of competitiveness involved – DON'T CHEAT – it will only end in tears.

The obvious way to cheat is to take a very subtle peep in the bag while (hopefully) your adversary is not looking – you can avoid this by insisting the bag stays above your shoulder when picking tiles. There are all sorts of house rules to combat any shenanigans, but in tournament play there have been several instances of players being banned when caught cheating.

In one event, the deathly hush of the playing area was interrupted by the organiser announcing in front of 200 people that someone had been found out – he was literally frogmarched out of the room by a security guard, never to be seen again…

Obviously, friendly games are a different matter, but if there's any potential of upsetting your opponent rather than humouring them, don't bother.

In any case bad karma will get you in the end.

**42** **Poker Face**

It can be easy to tell whether your opponent has a good or bad rack by the look on their face once they've picked their tiles, and they can give away where they want to play their next move by staring at a particular part of the board.

This doesn't matter too much in a friendly game but, if you want to win, it will help your cause to watch out for the giveaway signs, and not react to your own letters either facially or verbally.

You could actually try doing the opposite and, for example, moan when you get good letters, but that's when you get into gamesmanship and it's a little bit unnecessary, unless you think your opponent would do the same to you.

#  43 Know Your **Ologies**

Try studying these to some degree:

| | |
|---|---|
| **AEROLOGY** | study of the atmosphere |
| **AGROLOGY** | "    "    soils |
| **AREOLOGY** | Mars |
| **APIOLOGY** | bees |
| **BATOLOGY** | brambles |
| **CETOLOGY** | whales |
| **CHAOLOGY** | chaos theory |
| **DEMOLOGY** | demography |
| **DOXOLOGY** | short hymn |
| **ENOLOGY** | study of wine |
| **ETIOLOGY** | "    "    causes of diseases |
| **FETOLOGY** | the foetus |
| **MENOLOGY** | religious calendar |
| **MISOLOGY** | hatred of reasoned argument |
| **MIXOLOGY** | the art of mixing cocktails |
| **NOOLOGY** | study of intuition |
| **NOMOLOGY** | "    "    law |
| **NOSOLOGY** | classification of diseases |
| **OENOLOGY** | more wine |
| **OINOLOGY** | even more wine |
| **OOLOGY** | birds' eggs |
| **OREOLOGY** | mountains |
| **PEDOLOGY** | children |
| **PELOLOGY** | mud therapy |
| **PENOLOGY** | punishment |

| **RHEOLOGY** | matter in physics |
| **SEXOLOGY** | human sexual behaviour |
| **SINOLOGY** | Chinese culture |
| **SITOLOGY** | food |
| **UFOLOGY** | UFOs |
| **VINOLOGY** | vines |
| **VIROLOGY** | viruses |

**OLOGY** itself is also perfectly acceptable –
it has a rather less cerebral anagram.

# 44 Suffixes

Here are twenty combinations to look out for and put at the end of your rack since they are very fruitful suffixes:

-ABLE
-AGE
-ATE
-ED
-ER
-IC
-IEST
-ING
-ISM
-ISE

-ITE
-IVE
-IZE
-LESS
-LY
-MAN
-MEN
-NESS
-OUS
-TION

# 45 | Ess-ential

Apart from the blank, **S** is the best letter in the Scrabble set, since it starts and ends more words than any other. It should be savoured and ideally kept back to use in a bonus-word – certainly try not to use it unless you can score over 30 points. A good guide is to play it only if the score using it is at least 10 points more than the best score without.

Bear in mind though that multiple **S**s on your rack can hold you up. They're not as good together as you may think and if you have two it's normally best to offload one as soon as you can – you should still be able to achieve this with a decent score, but do hold the remaining one back for something special later.

# 46 Non-words

There's a multitude of surprisingly allowable **non**-words:

| | |
|---|---|
| **NONACTOR** | person who is not an actor |
| **NONBANK** | business providing similar services to a bank |
| **NONCOLA** | soft drink other than cola |
| **NONDRUG** | not involving use of drugs |
| **NONELITE** | not elite |
| **NONFUEL** | not relating to fuel |
| **NONGUILT** | innocence |
| **NONHARDY** | fragile |
| **NONIMAGE** | person who is not a celebrity |
| **NONJURY** | trial without a jury |
| **NONLEAFY** | not leafy |
| **NONMETRO** | not metropolitan |
| **NONNEWS** | not concerned with the news |
| **NONOILY** | not oily |
| **NONPARTY** | not connected with a political party |
| **NONQUOTA** | not included in a quota |
| **NONRIGID** | not rigid |
| **NONSELF** | foreign molecule in the body |
| **NONTIDAL** | not having a tide |
| **NONURBAN** | rural |
| **NONVITAL** | not vital |
| **NONWAGE** | not part of wages |
| **NONZERO** | not equal to zero |
| **NONWORDS** | is in the official Scrabble wordlist as well. |

**Play to the Board**

A common error among players is to spend all their time looking at their rack rather than the board. It's all very well spotting great words with the tiles in front of you but not much use if there's nowhere to place them. You're far better off spending 90% of your time focusing on the board and its possibilities, trying to keep your letters in your head simultaneously if you can.

Adapting to this '**visual switch**' is very important and can save you a lot of brain energy as well as improve your game. It's not a simple change to achieve, so keep consciously trying to 'catch yourself on' when overfocusing on your rack.

# 48 Blocking and Opening

**Block when ahead, open when behind.**
That's the general rule. However, you need to be careful you don't sacrifice too many points just to block, or you may find your lead diminishes sooner than you think. Likewise, you need to open up carefully and too small a score may leave your deficit too great.

Ideally, if you can block and score over 20 points simultaneously when ahead it's worth doing; if you're behind and can open the board for at least 15 points then go for it.

# 49 | Set-ups

Unlike chess where you have to think about twenty moves ahead, Scrabble is all about maximising your score over your current move as well as the potential score on the next move. This can be achieved with good **rack balancing** to edge you towards that elusive 50-point bonus word, and **set-up** plays.

If you have a high-scoring **J**, **Q**, **X** or **Z** for example, and nowhere really worthwhile to play it, you may be able to set up a big score next turn by placing one of your vowels next to a premium square. Alternatively, you could set up a **hook** by holding back a letter that goes on the beginning or end of the word you play.

For example, if you have **GHORTUZ**, it might be worth playing **ROUGH** keeping back the **T** for the front hook next time (it goes on the end as well) – even better if there is a premium square adjacent to the **O** of **ROUGH** to set up **ZO** for an alternative big score next time.

Try not to make the set-up too obvious though and play straight into the hands of your opponent. It's all about giving yourself future opportunities and when they come off it's extremely satisfying.

**By Hook or by Crook**

Knowing your **hooks** can give you a great advantage over your adversary. Here's an A to Z of great front hooks of 2-letter words:

| | | | |
|---|---|---|---|
| **A-ZO** | containing the divalent group N:N | **L-AH** | sixth degree of music scale |
| **B-OH** | exclamation to startle someone | **M-HO** | SI unit of conductance |
| **C-HE** | pronoun meaning 'I' | **N-OX** | nitrogen oxide |
| **D-IT** | to stop something happening | **O-BE** | Laconian village |
| | | **P-AX** | kiss of peace |
| **E-ME** | uncle | **Q-IS** | energies |
| **F-OY** | loyalty | **R-EM** | dose of radiation |
| **G-IF** | if | | |
| **H-EH** | exclamation of surprise | **S-HA** | be quiet |
| | | **T-EF** | African grass |
| **I-TA** | type of palm | **U-DO** | Japanese plant |
| **J-OR** | movement in Indian music | **V-IN** | French wine |
| | | **W-OF** | fool |
| **K-HI** | Greek letter | **X-IS** | Greek letters |
| | | **Y-GO** | past participle of 'go' |
| | | **Z-EL** | Turkish cymbal |

**Super Words**

There are also some wonderful words using the prefix **SUPER-**. Here are a few examples of 8-letter words that may help get you that elusive 50-point bonus (you can guess the definitions!):

| | |
|---|---|
| **SUPERBAD** | **SUPERHOT** |
| **SUPERCAR** | **SUPERJET** |
| **SUPERCOW** | **SUPERLOO** |
| **SUPERFAN** | **SUPERMOM** |
| **SUPERGUN** | **SUPERSPY** |

## 52 More Vowel Trouble

This list of 3-vowelled 4-letter words will solve your vowel-heavy rack problems quickly and save you scoring measly amounts for several turns in a row:

**AIGA** family
**AINE** male elder
**AITU** half-human half-divine being
**AJEE** awry
**ALAE** wings
**AMIA** fish
**AUNE** measure of length
**AWEE** for a short time
**EALE** Roman beast
**EAVE** to form eaves
**EINE** eyes
**EMEU** emu
**EOAN** relating to the dawn
**ETUI** small ornamented case
**EUGE** well done
**EVOE** cry of Bacchic frenzy
**HUIA** extinct New Zealand bird
**IDEE** idea
**ILIA** plural of 'ilium'
**IURE** by law

**KAIE** key
**MEOU** to meow
**MOAI** Easter Island stone figures
**MOOI** pleasing
**NAOI** ancient temples
**OBIA** a spell
**ODEA** buildings for musical performances
**OGEE** moulding
**OHIA** Hawaiian plant
**ONIE** any
**OUMA** grandmother
**OUPA** grandfather
**PAUA** New Zealand shellfish
**QUAI** quay
**TOEA** monetary unit of Papua New Guinea
**UNAI** two-toed sloth
**URAO** mineral
**UVEA** part of the eyeball
**VIAE** roads
**ZOEA** crab larva

# 53 Sub-mission

SUB- gives rise to some under-ful words:

| | |
|---|---|
| **SUBAREA** | area within a larger area |
| **SUBBREED** | breed within a larger breed |
| **SUBCOOL** | to make colder |
| **SUBDWARF** | star smaller than a dwarf star |
| **SUBERECT** | not quite erect |
| **SUBFLOOR** | rough floor |
| **SUBGOAL** | secondary goal |
| **SUBHEAD** | heading of a subsection |
| **SUBIDEA** | secondary idea |
| **SUBLEVEL** | subdivision of a level |
| **SUBMENU** | further options within computer menu |
| **SUBNICHE** | subdivision of a niche |
| **SUBOCEAN** | beneath the ocean |
| **SUBPANEL** | panel that is part of a larger panel |
| **SUBRACE** | a race considered to be inferior |
| **SUBSONG** | subdued birdsong |
| **SUBTUNIC** | garment worn under a tunic |
| **SUBUNIT** | distinct part of something larger |
| **SUBVICAR** | vicar's assistant |
| **SUBWORLD** | underworld |
| **SUBZONE** | subdivision of a zone |

## 54 It's Only a Game

At whatever level you're playing, it's easy to be a good winner but not so a good loser. Don't get too far away from the fact that Scrabble is fun.

There is nothing wrong with being competitive and wanting to win but, unless you really dislike your opponent, in which case you probably shouldn't be playing them in the first place, there's no reason to be a bad loser.

This is often a maturity issue and young players will grow out of it, hopefully sooner rather than later. Sometimes it helps to learn from a particularly painful defeat. When I played in the World Championship Final in 1999, I was beaten by just one point – it hurt badly and I didn't sleep properly for a year afterwards. Whenever I lose these days, I look back and think it can't be as bad as that, and that makes me lose better.

It really isn't worth getting too worked up over – keep things in perspective and enjoy the game whatever the outcome.

# 55 | Skulduggery

If you think your opponent is capable of some underhand tactics, try some of these to give them a taste of their own medicine:

(a) Make sure they are positioned in front of a mirror so you can see what's on their rack

(b) Party hard the night before and burp alcohol fumes over them

(c) Flick bogeys in the bag to put them off when picking their tiles

(d) Click your knuckles

(e) Cough a lot

(f) Eat lots of garlic

(g) Don't wash for a month before the game

(h) Hum

(i) Grind teeth

(j) Eat baked beans and cauliflower before the game and shoot off some silent-but-violents

I must thank my siblings for these suggestions – I would never have thought of them myself.

## 56 | Like-ability

It really is surprising how much the official Scrabble wordlist likes **-LIKE** as a suffix and it leads to loads of unlikely and useful words, for instance:

**AUNTLIKE**
**BAGLIKE**
**CAGELIKE**
**DUNELIKE**
**EARLIKE**
**FATLIKE**
**GATELIKE**
**HEADLIKE**
**IVYLIKE**
**JAWLIKE**
**LAVALIKE**

**MAPLIKE**
**NIBLIKE**
**OWLLIKE**
**PEALIKE**
**QUAYLIKE**
**RODLIKE**
**SAWLIKE**
**TEALIKE**
**URNLIKE**
**VASELIKE**
**WIGLIKE**

and I like **YLIKE** (a Spenserian form of alike).

## 57 | Je Ne Regrette Rien

Nothing can be more annoying than playing your turn and then spotting a better move that you could have played immediately after when it's too late – but there's a great skill in not compounding the mistake by dwelling on it.

Your mind should be fully focused on your current move and not hampered by wondering what might have been. I remember a Mastermind contestant who was doing brilliantly at the general knowledge round – he whizzed off ten answers in a row, then made one error which threw him completely and he got the next ten wrong.

It's much the same in Scrabble – far better to put mistakes out of your mind and move on.

## 58 | Have You Got What It Takes?

There are plenty of attributes that go into making a good Scrabble player. Numeracy, literacy, a sound mind, enthusiasm and positivity are just some of them. Experience counts a great deal too: like everything, practice makes perfect and the more you play, the more you'll improve.

A 'killer instinct' is important if you want to take it more seriously – I hope I'm not being too controversial by saying that this tends to be inbred in men more than women, but the reason the stats show that men seem to do better is that they generally have more time on their hands.

Top players are often creative mathematicians – this may seem contradictory as most people are either one or the other, but if you're lucky enough to be talented at both, you definitely have the basic ingredients to be a Scrabble success.

## 59 Juicy J-words

Here are twenty-five tasty treats using the **J**:

| | | | |
|---|---|---|---|
| **JA** | yes | **JEFE** | military leader |
| **JO** | sweetheart | **JEON** | Korean pancake |
| **GJU** | Shetland violin | **JIAO** | Chinese currency |
| **TAJ** | Muslim cap | | |
| **BAJU** | Malay jacket | **JIVY** | lively |
| **BENJ** | Indian hemp | **JOCO** | relaxed |
| **DOJO** | judo hall | **JOTA** | Spanish dance |
| **GAJO** | non-gypsy | **JUBE** | church gallery |
| **JAAP** | simpleton (*South African offensive*) | **JYNX** | woodpecker |
| | | **FALAJ** | water channel |
| **JAGA** | to guard | **KANJI** | Japanese writing system |
| **JAKE** | all right | | |
| **JAXY** | buttocks | **LAPJE** | rag |
| **JEAT** | jet | **PUNJI** | bamboo stick |

Ideally you'll be looking to use the **J** in conjunction with one of the premium squares, and scoring around thirty points in the process if the board is relatively open.

# 60 | Jinn and Tonic

**JINN** is a spirit (not the drink) in Muslim mythology, but it can be spelt in several different ways:

**DJIN**
**DJINN**
**DJINNI**
**DJINNY**

**GINN**
**JINNEE**
**JINNI**

Of these, only **DJIN**, **DJINN** and **JINNI** take an **S** for some reason.

To confuse you further, also allowable are **JIN** – a Chinese unit of weight – and **JINNE**, which is a South African exclamation of surprise.

# 61 | Q without a U

The **Q** can really cramp your style during the game and it's really not worth holding on to in the hope that you pick up a **U** further down the line. However, as well as the invaluable **QI**, there are some more wonderful U-less **Q** words. These are the most useful ones:

| | |
|---|---|
| **QAT** | African shrub |
| **QIN** | Chinese musical instrument |
| **CINQ** | number five |
| **FIQH** | Islamic jurisprudence |
| **QADI** | Muslim judge |
| **QAID** | chief |
| **QOPH** | Hebrew letter |
| **WAQF** | Muslim endowment |
| **FAQIR** | Muslim who spurns worldly possessions |
| **NIQAB** | Muslim veil |
| **QANAT** | underground channel |
| **QIBLA** | direction of Mecca |
| **QORMA** | mild Indian dish |
| **TALAQ** | Muslim divorce |
| **TRANQ** | tranquilizer |
| **NIQAAB** | Muslim veil |
| **QABALA** | Jewish mystical tradition |
| **QASIDA** | Arabic verse form |
| **QIGONG** | system of breathing and exercise |
| **QINDAR** | Albanian monetary unit |
| **QINTAR** | Albanian monetary unit |
| **QWERTY** | keyboard |
| **SHEQEL** | Israeli monetary unit (*plural*) |
| **YAQONA** | Polynesian shrub |
| **INQILAB** | revolution |

## 62 X-pertise

The **X** is the best of the high-scorers, largely because it goes with all the vowels to make 2-letter words:

**AX**  axe
**EX**  to delete
**XI**  Greek letter
**OX**
**XU**  Vietnamese currency

Always look to play it on the doubles and triples – doubling up both ways can bring you an easy thirty-two or tripling gets you forty-eight points just for the **X** alone.

Here are some 3-letter **X**-amples to help you **X**-cel:

**DEX**  dextroamphetamine
**DUX**  top school pupil
**GOX**  gaseous oxygen
**HOX**  hamstring
**KEX**  plant
**LEX**  system of laws
**LOX**  to load with liquid oxygen
**MUX**  to spoil
**OXY**  ox
**PIX**  receptacle

**PYX**  receptacle
**REX**  king
**TEX**  weight unit measuring yarn density
**TIX**  tickets
**TUX**  tuxedo
**VOX**  voice
**WEX**  to wax
**WOX**  wax
**YEX**  to hiccup

# 63 Zo Far Zo Good

The infamous **ZO** – officially a Tibetan breed of cattle formed by crossing a yak with a cow – has ten other members of its herd:

**DSO**
**DSOBO**
**DSOMO**
**DZO**
**DZHO**
**JOMO**
**ZHO**
**ZHOMO**
**ZOBO**
**ZOBU**

Note well that the **DSOMO** and **ZHOMO** are female, while the **ZEBU** – an Asian ox with a humped back – can be seen grazing in the next field.

## 64   Enjoy the Moment

When you happen to spot a fantastic word or a game-winning move, just take a minute or so to savour the satisfaction, rather than play it immediately.

The uplifting feeling will seep through you – you don't have to jump in the air or do handstands – just sit back and relax in your good vibe, whilst your opponent has absolutely no idea what's coming.

# 65 South African Words

Lots of South African entries have reached the official Scrabble wordlist in the last few years, for example:

| | |
|---|---|
| **BRU** | a friend |
| **JOL** | to have a good time |
| **SIF** | nasty |
| **BOEP** | protruding belly |
| **BOET** | brother |
| **BRAK** | crossbred dog |
| **EISH** | expressing dismay |
| **ISIT** | seeking confirmation |
| **KAAL** | naked |
| **KIFF** | excellent |
| **MOER** | to attack someone |
| **WENA** | you |
| **YEBO** | yes |
| **BRAAI** | to grill over open coals |
| **NOOIT** | expressing surprise |
| **SPAZA** | township shop (*slang*) |
| **VOEMA** | vigour |

**More Hooks**

There are loads of handy front hooks of 3-letter words to make some really weird 4-letter words – here's just a sample:

| | | | |
|---|---|---|---|
| **S-AXE** | greyish-blue colour | **G-LEG** | quick |
| **K-BAR** | kilobar | **S-MEW** | a duck |
| **E-COD** | expression of surprise | **E-NOW** | enough |
| **U-DON** | Japanese noodles | **Y-OWE** | ewe |
| **T-EGG** | two-year-old sheep | **A-POD** | animal without feet |
| **V-EGO** | vegetarian | **E-REV** | day before |
| **M-EVE** | to move | **V-ROT** | rotten |
| **A-GIN** | against | **V-ROW** | woman |
| **P-HAT** | terrific | **E-SKY** | food and drink container |
| **Z-ILL** | finger cymbal | **E-THE** | easy |
| **J-IMP** | handsome | **O-URN** | our |
| **T-IVY** | at full speed | **E-VET** | newt |
| **S-JOE** | exclamation of surprise | **H-WAN** | won |
| **K-LAP** | to slap | **H-YEN** | hyena |
| | | **P-YET** | magpie |
| | | **M-ZEE** | old person |

# 67  A Young Man's Game?

Eleven of the twelve World Scrabble Champions have been single men under 40-years old. Joel Wapnick from Canada gives hope to us all – he won the title at the age of 53 – but there's no denying agile young minds have an advantage. The best young players are from Thailand as Scrabble is included in their school curriculum as a way of teaching English. It would be lovely to see a greater Scrabble presence in UK schools as it's such a fun way to improve children's literacy and numeracy.

There are a few youth workshops and competitions over here. Having personally taught in several lunchtime and after-school clubs, I can say that the enthusiasm is tremendous. A word of advice however to the youngsters from a wise old man: 'don't be too cocky and slow down a bit'.

## 68 More Corkers

Another alphabet of absolute beauties:

| | |
|---|---|
| **ADZUKI** | leguminous plant |
| **BLIPVERT** | very short television advertisement |
| **CHILIDOG** | hot dog with chilli sauce |
| **DRONKLAP** | drunkard |
| **EXEQUY** | funeral rite |
| **FJELD** | high rocky Scandinavian plateau |
| **GILLYVOR** | carnation |
| **HRYVNIA** | money unit of Ukraine |
| **IZVESTIA** | news |
| **JEDI** | person claiming to live according to Star Wars Jedi philosophy |
| **KUVASZ** | Hungarian dog |
| **LOGJUICE** | poor quality port |
| **MPRET** | former Albanian ruler |
| **NONG** | stupid person (*Australian slang*) |
| **OULAKAN** | fish |
| **PYENGADU** | leguminous tree |
| **QUANDONG** | small Australian tree |
| **RUBABOO** | soup |
| **STINKPOT** | person that stinks |
| **TAKIN** | massive S. Asian mammal with shaggy coat and backwards and upwards horns |

| | |
|---|---|
| **UINTAITE** | asphalt |
| **VOZHD** | Russian leader |
| **WAYLEGGO** | 'away here! let go!' |
| **XENOPUS** | African frog |
| **YUTZ** | fool |
| **ZELATRIX** | nun monitoring younger nuns' behaviour |

## 69 | Hard of Herring

**-FISH** is another swimmingly seaworthy suffix when you trawl through the official Scrabble wordlist:

| | |
|---|---|
| **BATFISH** | **MILKFISH** |
| **CAVEFISH** | **NUMBFISH** |
| **DEALFISH** | **OARFISH** |
| **FOOLFISH** | **PANFISH** |
| **GOATFISH** | **ROSEFISH** |
| **HEADFISH** | **STUDFISH** |
| **JEWFISH** | **TUBFISH** |
| **LADYFISH** | **WEAKFISH** |

The de-fin-itions are not in plaice: they're all types of fish.

# 70 Tile Tracking

Tracking tiles is allowable and really important if you want to get more serious. It helps to give you a rough idea of consonant to vowel ratio as the game goes on. If you find more consonants than normal have already been played for example, you may want to play less on your turn as there are comparatively less left in the bag to pick – this is really useful when it comes to balancing your rack.

However, the main point of tracking is in the endgame, especially if the scores are close. If you track correctly – which is surprisingly simple with a bit of practice – you will know what's on your opponent's rack once the bag is emptied. This allows you to spot what you think is their best move and stop them in their tracks by blocking appropriately, which could make all the difference between winning and losing.

All you need to do to tile track is write out the alphabet at the start of the game and cross off the letters as they are played. For example, if **MARK** is played on the first move, write down 8 next to your **A** as there will be eight **A**'s left unplayed. Similarly 1 next to the **M**, 5 next to the **R** and delete the **K** completely.

If you keep going, and cross out your own rack once the bag is empty, you should be left with exactly what's on your opponent's rack.

## 71 | **Check Your Averages**

You can get a good idea as to how fast your game is improving by working out your average score per (two-player) game – even more useful is finding your average move score.

As a rough guide, you're doing well if you score 300, while 300–350 will see you hold your own at a club, and 350–400 will stand you in good stead at an event. The top players average 400–450.

Scores can vary dramatically depending on the state of the board (open or blocked) and the quality of opponent, which is why average move score is a better indicator. Aim for over 20 points per move – 25 is really good and 30 is excellent.

Doing this can give you a good feel for what to look for from each turn. For instance, if you can only find a score less than 20 points, it might be worth considering changing your letters unless the ones you hold back are so good that you're likely to make up for it with a score of 30–40 on the next turn.

# UK OK

The odd one out of **ENGLAND**, **IRELAND**, **SCOTLAND** and **WALES** is **IRELAND**, as it's the only one not to have an anagram – surprising with such common letters.

| | | |
|---|---|---|
| **ENGLAND** | **ENDLANG** | lengthways |
| **SCOTLAND** | **COTLANDS** | cotter's grounds |
| **WALES** | **ALEWS** | hunting cries |
| | **SWALE** | to sway |
| | **SWEAL** | to scorch |
| | **WEALS** | raised skin marks |

However, **IRELAND** does go with the following letters to make an 8-letter word:

| | | |
|---|---|---|
| +B | **BILANDER** | small cargo ship |
| +E | **RENAILED** | |
| +F | **FILANDER** | kangaroo |
| +G | **DANGLIER** | |
| +G | **DEARLING** | |
| +G | **DRAGLINE** | |
| +H | **HARDLINE** | |
| +N | **INLANDER** | |
| +S | **ISLANDER** | |

There's a plethora of Maori words in the official Scrabble wordlist – here are some really useful fours:

| | |
|---|---|
| **HAKU** | the kingfish |
| **HAPU** | a subtribe |
| **HIOI** | plant of the mint family |
| **HOKA** | red cod |
| **KARO** | small shrub |
| **KAWA** | protocol |
| **KETE** | basket |
| **KOHA** | gift |
| **KORU** | carving pattern |
| **KUIA** | elderly woman |
| **KUTU** | body louse |
| **MIHA** | young fern |
| **MIHI** | to greet ceremonially |
| **MIRO** | coniferous tree |
| **NAMU** | black sandfly |
| **PATU** | short club |
| **PUHA** | sow thistle |
| **PUKA** | tobacco plant |
| **WERO** | challenge |
| **WHIO** | blue duck |

**More Maori**

Here's a top twenty of Maori fives – they can often
get you out of vowel trouble:

| | |
|---|---|
| **AINGA** | village |
| **ARIKI** | first-born child |
| **AROHA** | love |
| **HIKOI** | to protest |
| **HINAU** | tree |
| **KANAE** | grey mullet |
| **KAURU** | edible cabbage stem |
| **KAWAU** | black shag |
| **KEHUA** | ghost |
| **KIORE** | rat |
| **KOURA** | crayfish |
| **MAPAU** | small tree |
| **MATAI** | evergreen tree |
| **MAURI** | the soul |
| **MOHUA** | small bird |
| **PIKAU** | rucksack |
| **POTAE** | hat |
| **RAHUI** | prohibition |
| **RAUPO** | bulrush |
| **TAWAI** | beech |

**Type-cast**

There are several kinds of words with the **-TYPE** suffix:

| | |
|---|---|
| **AUTOTYPE** | photographic process |
| **BIOTYPE** | genetically identical plant group |
| **CEROTYPE** | printing plate process |
| **ECOTYPE** | group of organisms |
| **GENOTYPE** | genetic constitution of organism |
| **HOLOTYPE** | original specimen |
| **IDIOTYPE** | unique part of antibody |
| **KALOTYPE** | early photographic process |
| **LINOTYPE** | line of metal type |
| **MONOTYPE** | single print |
| **NEOTYPE** | replacement specimen |
| **OVERTYPE** | to type over existing text |
| **PRETYPE** | to type in advance |
| **SEROTYPE** | category into which bacterium is placed |
| **TINTYPE** | photographic print |
| **VARITYPE** | to produce copy |
| **ZOOTYPE** | animal figure used as a symbol |

## 76 Never Say Never

Don't give up if you find yourself a long way behind; part of the beauty of Scrabble is there's nearly always the opportunity to turn it around.

When I was playing in the World Championship Final, I was 177 down and came back to win by 7 points to make the match score 2–2. My opponent was so downhearted that the deciding game was a breeze. Keep positive and believe the 'tile gods' will ultimately favour you – you'll be surprised how often they do.

**77** **Off the Record**

If you are really keen, you could put down all sorts of wordlists on tape and play them back to yourself with some uplifting background music. You'll be surprised how many will subconsciously stick.

But beware: this form of practice can be highly dangerous. You would think that long car journeys would be an ideal opportunity to make use of this method, but in my experience you have a high chance of falling asleep at the wheel. Therefore, playback time might be best left for going to bed; it's a great cure for insomnia if nothing else.

## 78 Special Sixes

If you're ahead in the game, there are some great 6-letter words that are especially useful in acting as blockers as they don't take any hooks at either end. Also, the more letters you play when in front, the sooner you get to the finishing line. Here's an alphabet of examples:

| | | | |
|---|---|---|---|
| **ARGULI** | parasites on fish | **MONOAO** | New Zealand plant |
| **BONZER** | excellent | **NOGAKU** | Japanese drama |
| **CHANGA** | expression of approval | **OCHONE** | expression of regret |
| **DADGUM** | damned | **PLONGD** | plunged |
| **EQUALI** | pieces for instruments | **QUOOKE** | quaked |
| **FOOBAR** | irreparably damaged | **RAWARU** | New Zealand cod |
| **GATVOL** | fed up | **SHAZAM** | magic slogan |
| **HUPIRO** | offensive-smelling tree | **TIGLIC** | syrupy liquid |
| **IBIDEM** | in the same place | **UBIQUE** | everywhere |
| **JANTEE** | sprightly | **VERLIG** | enlightened |
| **KERERU** | New Zealand pigeon | **WABBIT** | weary |
| **LIKUTA** | Zaire coin | **XOANON** | carved image of a god |
| | | **YITTEN** | frightened |
| | | **ZAFTIG** | curvaceous |

They have the added advantage of potentially lulling your opponent into a mistake by putting an **S** on the end and thereby losing a turn.

# 79 Magnificent Sevens

**ETAERIO** – a kind of fruit – is the most likely 7-letter bonus word to appear on your rack. Here's a taster of some more fruitful 7-letter words made up of the letters you are most likely to draw: **ADEILNORST**. They are especially useful when they have no anagram and are listed here in order of probability of being drawn:

| | | | |
|---|---|---|---|
| **ERASION** | act of erasing | **RIOTISE** | riotous behaviour |
| **ATONIES** | lack of muscle tone | **ALIENER** | one who transfers |
| **EROTISE** | to make erotic | **EATERIE** | restaurant |
| | | **ARENOSE** | sandy |
| **AIERIES** | eagles' nests | **OLEATES** | salts of oleic acid |
| **TAENIAE** | ancient Greek headbands | | |
| | | **TORNADE** | tornado |
| **INOSITE** | alcohol | **NEROLIS** | oils used in perfumery |
| **ROSEATE** | rose-coloured | **AEOLIAN** | relating to the wind |
| **SEALINE** | sailing company | **OREADES** | mountain nymphs |
| **SENARII** | poems | **SIENITE** | igneous rock |
| **ANISOLE** | colourless liquid | **INEDITA** | unpublished writings |
| **ESTRONE** | hormone | **AEROSAT** | communications satellite |
| **OLEARIA** | daisy bush | | |

**AERATION** – putting gas into a liquid – is the most commonly played 8-letter word in Scrabble. You'll be surprised how often the following words appear if you hold the right bonus-conducive letters back:

| | |
|---|---|
| **INERTIAE** | a plural of 'inertia' |
| **ERIONITE** | glassy mineral |
| **AEROLITE** | meteorite |
| **AEROTONE** | bath with air jets |
| **ERADIATE** | radiate |
| **DENTARIA** | botanical term |
| **DOUANIER** | customs officer |
| **TENORITE** | black mineral |
| **TAENIATE** | ribbon-like |
| **ETIOLATE** | to become weak |
| **LITERATO** | literary person |
| **TENTORIA** | membranes |
| **RETAILOR** | to tailor afresh |
| **ORIENTED** | orientated |
| **AURELIAN** | person who studies butterflies |
| **DELATION** | bringing a charge against |
| **INAURATE** | gilded |
| **NOTITIAE** | ecclesiastical registers |
| **ETOURDIE** | foolish |
| **RITORNEL** | orchestral passage |
| **RETINOID** | vitamin A derivative |
| **TERATOID** | like a monster |
| **INTORTED** | twisted inward |
| **TRIENNIA** | periods of three years |

## 81 Even More Hooks

Here are thirty bizarre end hooks to normal 3-letter words that make perfectly valid 4s:

| | | | |
|---|---|---|---|
| **BAG-H** | garden | **PAW-A** | peacock |
| **BED-U** | relating to bedouins | **PUT-Z** | to waste time |
| **COX-A** | hipbone | **ROT-L** | Muslim unit of weight |
| **DID-O** | antic | | |
| **FEE-B** | contemptible person | **SEX-T** | noon |
| | | **SIT-Z** | bath |
| **FIX-T** | fixed | **TOY-O** | Japanese material for making hats |
| **GEE-Z** | expression of surprise | | |
| **GET-A** | Japanese sandal | **TRY-E** | very good |
| | | **UPS-Y** | drunken merry-making |
| **HER-Y** | to praise | | |
| **IMP-I** | group of Zulu warriors | **VAN-G** | rope on ship |
| | | **VAT-U** | monetary unit of Vanuatu |
| **JAM-B** | to climb a crack in a rock | | |
| | | **WAD-T** | wad |
| **KIP-E** | basket for catching fish | **WET-A** | wingless insect |
| **LIP-O** | liposuction | **YES-K** | to hiccup |
| **MAR-Y** | marijuana | **YOU-K** | to itch |
| **NAB-K** | edible berry | **ZIT-I** | pasta |

# Even More Vowel Trouble

These 4-vowelled 5-letter words are rare in normal English but extremely useful in Scrabble:

| | |
|---|---|
| **AECIA** | structures in fungi |
| **AERIE** | eagle's nest |
| **AQUAE** | waters |
| **AULOI** | ancient Greek pipes |
| **AURAE** | a plural of 'aura' |
| **AUREI** | Roman coins |
| **LOOIE** | lieutenant |
| **LOUIE** | " |
| **MIAOU** | to meow |
| **OORIE** | shabby |
| **OUIJA** | spirit board |
| **OURIE** | shabby |
| **URAEI** | sacred Egyptian serpents |
| **ZOAEA** | crab larva |
| **ZOOEA** | "    " |

## 83 | Triple Tactics

The triple-word squares – TWS – are the most bountiful on the board when it comes to points potential. When one becomes available it's often the place to play, but don't get too transfixed by a triple. Some opportunities are better than others depending on your letters. So think very carefully before playing a vowel immediately adjacent to a TWS, but placing a low scoring consonant on the triple line isn't as dangerous as you might think.

Your opponent might score thirty or so points off it, but that's worth the risk if your triple opening move scores far better than any other on the board. You might get unlucky and let them in for a big fifty plus score, or in the worst-case scenario a **triple-triple** or **'9-timer'**, where they place their seven letters around the one you've put on the triple line to take in two TWS's for a mammoth move – I once scored 311 with **CONQUEST**. This, however, occurs very rarely and the trick is not to be too paranoid.

So weigh up the odds when opening a TWS – it's worth doing if your score outweighs the give away potential.

If it's your move and a TWS is available, it's the first place you look for, but if you can't make the most of it, don't be afraid to look elsewhere – your opponent may not be able to use it effectively either. An interesting tactic in this instance is to open up a second TWS so you get a share of the spoils on your next turn – risky but fun.

## 84 | Handy Hindi

There are plenty of Delhi-cious short words originating from India:

| | | | |
|---|---|---|---|
| **DAK** | mail | **GORI** | white female (*Hinglish Informal*) |
| **GHI** | ghee | | |
| **JAI** | victory | **KHUD** | ravine |
| **REH** | salty crust on soil | **KUTA** | male dog |
| | | **KUTI** | female dog |
| **SER** | unit of weight | **LAKH** | 100,000 |
| **URD** | bean | **LEEP** | to plaster with cow-dung |
| **ANNA** | coin | | |
| **ARNA** | water buffalo | **MALA** | string of beads used in prayer |
| **ARTI** | religious ritual | | |
| **BABU** | Mister | **MOTI** | fat woman |
| **BAEL** | spiny tree | **MOWA** | tree |
| **BAPU** | spiritual father | **NACH** | dance |
| **BHUT** | ghost | **NALA** | ravine |
| **BUDA** | old man | **PICE** | coin |
| **BUDI** | old woman | **RYOT** | peasant |
| **CHIK** | a blind | **SANT** | devout person |
| **DESI** | authentic | **TEEK** | well |
| **DHOL** | drum | **YAAR** | friend |
| **GORA** | white male (*Hinglish Informal*) | **ZILA** | administrative district |

# 85 More Handy Hindi

Have a Goa at these Indian fives:

| | |
|---|---|
| **AARTI** | ceremony with lighted candles |
| **BAJRA** | cereal grass |
| **BUNDH** | strike |
| **BEEDI** | hand-rolled cigarette |
| **BIGHA** | land measure |
| **CHOLI** | blouse |
| **DHUTI** | loincloth |
| **DURZI** | tailor |
| **GOSHT** | meat dish |
| **JAGRA** | festival |
| **JOWAR** | grass |
| **KHADI** | cotton cloth |
| **LUNGI** | long cloth |
| **MANDI** | big market |
| **PIPUL** | fig tree |
| **RATHA** | carriage |
| **SWAMI** | mystic |
| **TAVAH** | frying pan |
| **THAGI** | thuggery |
| **TONGA** | two-wheeled vehicle |
| **YOJAN** | unit of distance |

## 86 | Rising to the Challenge

Apart from some of the major events where there's a 5-point penalty, you've got nothing to lose in UK Scrabble by challenging a word you don't know, whereas in the US you lose your next turn if the word turns out to be OK. There's something aesthetically unpleasing about non-words staying on the board, but it's surprising how often it happens. **Don't be afraid to challenge**: if you have a scintilla of doubt, look it up. There's nothing more frustrating than letting a word go and finding it's not in the dictionary when it's too late. It might seem obvious when the challenges are 'free', but it's surprising how often players feel too embarrassed or intimidated to check.

As a general rule, challenge anything you wouldn't be sure of playing yourself.

## Vanquish the V

**V**s are horrible and should be discarded at the earliest opportunity. Here are forty voluptuous 3- and 4-letter **V**-words to assist you:

| | |
|---|---|
| **DEV** | divine being |
| **EVO** | evening |
| **LUV** | love |
| **SAV** | saveloy |
| **UVA** | grape |
| **VAC** | to vacuum |
| **VAV** | Hebrew letter |
| **VAW** | Hebrew letter |
| **VIG** | interest on loan |
| **VOE** | small bay |
| **VOL** | volume |
| **VOR** | to warn |
| **VUG** | small rock cavity |
| **VUM** | to swear |
| **GYVE** | to shackle |
| **KAVA** | Polynesian shrub |
| **OMOV** | 'one member, one vote' |
| **RIVO** | informal toast |
| **TAVA** | Indian frying pan |
| **ULVA** | seaweed |
| **VAGI** | cranial nerves |
| **VANG** | rope on ship |
| **VAUT** | vault |

| | |
|---|---|
| **VEEP** | vice president |
| **VEHM** | medieval German court |
| **VERD** | marble |
| **VEXT** | vexed |
| **VIBS** | climbing shoes |
| **VILD** | vile |
| **VITE** | musical direction |
| **VIVA** | to examine in a spoken interview |
| **VIVE** | long live |
| **VIVO** | with vigour |
| **VIZY** | to look |
| **VLEI** | low marshy ground |
| **VOLK** | nation |
| **VRIL** | life force |
| **VROU** | woman |
| **VUGH** | small rock cavity |
| **VULN** | to wound |

**U Don't Want to Be with a W**

Two letters that are awful together are the **U** and **W** – there are a few words to help get rid of them both in one turn:

| | |
|---|---|
| **WUD** | wood |
| **WUS** | term of address |
| **WAUK** | full cloth |
| **WAUL** | to cry like a cat |
| **WAUR** | war |
| **WHUP** | to defeat totally |
| **WUDU** | ritual washing |
| **WULL** | will |
| **DWAUM** | to faint |
| **SWOUN** | swoon |
| **UNWED** | not wed |
| **UNWET** | not wet |
| **UNWIT** | to divest of wit |
| **UNWON** | not won |
| **VROUW** | woman |
| **WAUFF** | to flutter |
| **WAUGH** | to bark |
| **WAULK** | full cloth |
| **WHUMP** | to make a dull thud |
| **WOFUL** | woeful |
| **WURST** | large sausage |
| **WUSHU** | Chinese martial arts |
| **WUSSY** | feeble |
| **WUXIA** | Chinese film |

# 89 Off the Hook

There are some surprising hooks you can play on the end of regular 2-letter words as well:

| | | | |
|---|---|---|---|
| **GO-A** | Tibetan gazelle | **WE-M** | womb |
| **MI-B** | a marble | **GO-N** | geometrical grade |
| **TO-C** | signal for letter T | **EX-O** | excellent |
| **LO-D** | logarithm | **HE-P** | hip |
| **HI-E** | to hurry | **LA-R** | young man |
| **DO-F** | stupid | **BY-S** | byes |
| **ME-G** | megabyte | **AT-T** | Siamese coin |
| **NO-H** | Japanese drama | **AM-U** | unit of mass |
| **MO-I** | me | **PA-V** | pavlova |
| **HA-J** | Muslim pilgrimage | **MA-W** | to bite |
| **TA-K** | take | **SO-X** | socks |
| **DO-L** | unit of pain intensity | **HO-Y** | to drive animal with cry |
| | | **RE-Z** | reservation |

The only 3-letter word ending in **Q** is **SUQ** – a Muslim market place – sadly this isn't a hook as **SU** isn't a word, but it's still extremely useful.

## 90 Angry Words

**ANGRIEST** is the most productive 8-letter anagram combination:

| | |
|---|---|
| **ANGSTIER** | more anxious |
| **ASTRINGE** | to cause contraction |
| **GANISTER** | sedimentary rock |
| **GANTRIES** | |
| **GRANITES** | |
| **INGRATES** | ungrateful people |
| **RANGIEST** | |
| **REASTING** | being noisily uncooperative |
| **STEARING** | steering |
| **TASERING** | using a Taser gun |

It's not that important to know all the anagrams – the more the better – but if you know two or three, you're more than likely to be able to fit one of them on the board.

# 91 Wise Words

A few **-WISE** words to end our suffix sojourn:

| | |
|---|---|
| **ARCHWISE** | like an arch |
| **BENDWISE** | diagonally |
| **CRABWISE** | sideways |
| **DROPWISE** | in form of a drop |
| **EDGEWISE** | edgeways |
| **FANWISE** | like a fan |
| **LONGWISE** | lengthways |
| **MANWISE** | in a human way |
| **OVERWISE** | too wise |
| **PALEWISE** | by perpendicular lines |
| **RINGWISE** | experienced in the ring |
| **SOMEWISE** | to some degree |
| **TENTWISE** | in the manner of a tent |
| **WARPWISE** | in the direction of the warp |

Interestingly, **WISEMAN** is not allowed but
**WISEWOMAN** is – it means a witch.

# 92 ⫿ Fatherly Advice

**PATERNAL** has two appropriate anagrams – **PARENTAL** and **PRENATAL** – speaking of which there's also **PARLANTE**.

Is this coincidence or is there more to it? When you consider that the following are also anagrams of one another –

'ELEVEN PLUS TWO' and 'TWELVE PLUS ONE'

'APPLE MACINTOSH' and 'LAPTOP MACHINES'

'THE HOUSES OF PARLIAMENT' and 'LOONIES FAR UP THE THAMES'

– and the fact that the only time I've ever, in tens of thousands of games, played **NY** and **MAN** in the same move, was in the World Championship Final – in New York… you start to wonder – well I certainly do.

# 93 | ZZZS

Respect your opponent by not playing too slowly. A good average time to play each move is about two minutes. In tournament play, special timers are used and you're allowed twenty-five minutes to play all your moves – since each game lasts an average of about thirteen moves each, you're looking at just under two minutes for each turn.

Some moves are more difficult than others, so it's fair enough to take longer sometimes, but anything in excess of five minutes and you're likely to send your opponent to sleep. The only time I have ever played my wife I dropped off due to her slow play and we never finished the game.

If you use a timer, the rule is that you lose 10 points for every minute (or part thereof) that you go over the twenty-five minute deadline. There was a rather elderly chap in the States who was 250 points ahead in his game, when he started snoring – his devious opponent realised his only chance of winning was to let him stay asleep and the poor man apparently went over on his timer by twenty-five minutes. He woke up to find that his 250-point lead had been cancelled out, but just in time to play the winning move: justice done.

By the way **ZZZS** is actually a valid word – the last in the official Scrabble wordlist – though you'd have to use both blanks to play it as there's only one **Z** in the set.

**Hook, Line, and Sinker**

The final word on the hooks is left to these fabulous front hooks of 7-letter words to make fantastic 8s:

| | |
|---|---|
| **A-DUSTING** | drying up by heat |
| **B-ARTISAN** | small turret |
| **C-UNIFORM** | ancient writing system |
| **D-HURRIES** | Indian cotton carpet |
| **E-RODENTS** | things that wear away |
| **F-UGLIEST** | extremely ugly |
| **G-ELASTIC** | relating to laughter |
| **H-EXAMINE** | type of fuel |
| **I-CONICAL** | relating to an icon |
| **J-AUNTIES** | naval masters-at-arms |
| **K-VETCHES** | grumbles |
| **L-IGNEOUS** | like wood |
| **M-UNITING** | strengthening |
| **N-OVATION** | substitution of a new obligation |
| **O-DONATES** | dragonflies |
| **P-LUMBAGO** | plant |
| **R-ENFORCE** | reinforce |
| **S-CHILLER** | unusual mineral lustre |
| **T-HERMITS** | processes for reducing metallic oxides |
| **U-PLAYING** | stashing |
| **V-ROOMING** | moving noisily at high speed |
| **W-INDIGOS** | cannibals |
| **Y-EARLIES** | once a year events |
| **Z-INKIEST** | most like zinc |

**Superstitions**

You don't need to wear 666 across your forehead or bring in a black cat, but if you think a certain superstition brings you luck, use it – for the power of positive thinking if nothing else.

When I won the World Championship, I found I was on a winning run after using the same toilet cubicle in between games – I would go through the same routine every time, but it became rather embarrassing when someone was already in there and I hung around the bathroom waiting for them to finish – I remember getting several strange looks from other users of the facilities.

Even so, anything that gives you a good vibe is worth pursuing. It could be as simple as deciding that **AMIGO** is a better move than its anagram **IMAGO**, just because it's more friendly.

# Do You Feel Lucky?

Part of the beauty of Scrabble is that, with some good fortune, nearly anyone can beat anyone. However, luck does not play as big a part in the game as you might think. It is no coincidence that the weakest players are the ones who tend to blame their luck the most.

Nigel Richards, multiple World Champion and regarded by many as the best player in the world, never curses his luck. He has won countless tournaments and almost invariably features in the top five of any event. Skill in Scrabble far outweighs fortune. The more you moan about your letters, the worse they are likely to get – negativity breeds negativity so avoid it at all costs.

You can certainly **make your own luck** in the game by giving yourself opportunities that others might not spot – it doesn't pay off all the time, but it will count in the long run.

The biggest luck element comes in picking up most of the blanks and **S**s – the best tiles in the set. Even then, you can increase your chances of getting these by simply playing more letters than your opponent, which is a skill in itself.

Over a lot of games, the better players always rise to the top, but if you're evenly matched, a little bit of luck can make all the difference.

Every five years or so, the official Scrabble wordlist is updated. The latest edition contains over 3000 new words up to eight letters in length which are recognised in official tournament play.

Forty fabulous new favourites follow:

| | |
|---|---|
| **BAHOOKIE** | the buttocks |
| **BARFI** | Indian dessert |
| **BIMINI** | awning for a yacht |
| **BODYMAN** | person who repairs car bodies |
| **CAMCORD** | film with a camcorder |
| **CINQ** | the number five |
| **COOLIST** | person who does not believe in global warming |
| **DHIKR** | Sufi religious ceremony |
| **DIDDUMS** | expression of sympathy to a child |
| **EARHOLE** | the external opening of the ear |
| **EEEW** | exclamation of disgust |
| **EQUES** | horseman in ancient Rome |
| **EZINE** | magazine in electronic form |
| **FOO** | temporary variable in computing |
| **GRIZ** | grizzly bear |
| **INDEEDY** | indeed |
| **MANBAG** | handbag carried by men |
| **MARGATE** | fish of the West Atlantic |
| **MIGAWD** | expression of surprise |

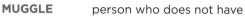

| | |
|---|---|
| **MUGGLE** | person who does not have supernatural powers |
| **NAV** | navigation |
| **NOCEBO** | substance causing harmful effects if patients expect it to be harmful |
| **NUG** | lump of wood sawn from a log |
| **OBVS** | obviously |
| **ONESIE** | one-piece garment combining a top with trousers |
| **PACZKI** | round filled doughnut |
| **PEPSI** | brand of soft drink |
| **POLYBAG** | put into a polythene bag |
| **RODNEY** | small fishing boat used in Canada |
| **RUGRAT** | young child |
| **SCUMBALL** | contemptible person |
| **SEIZA** | traditional Japanese kneeling position |
| **SICKY** | day off work due to illness |
| **STINGE** | miserly person |
| **TIZ** | state of confusion |
| **VAPE** | inhale from an electronic cigarette |
| **VIDIOT** | person who watches low-quality television |
| **WATCHA** | greeting meaning 'what are you?' |
| **WOJUS** | of poor quality |
| **XED** | marked a cross against |

## 98 | Eliminate the Page

If you are enthusiastic enough to look at some wordlists, a good way to study is to remove the words you are sure you have mastered by deleting them with a black marker pen.

Each time you go back to the relevant page, you'll be able to remove more by recognition, so it will continually seem less daunting to study until you ultimately eliminate the whole page – this is a very satisfying and positive way to learn and move on.

**Consonant Dumps**

If you hold six or seven consonants on your rack, you'll be looking to restore the balance.

These 2- and 3-letter consonant-only words will help:

| | |
|---|---|
| **CH** | eke |
| **FY** | fie |
| **KY** | cows |
| **NY** | nigh |
| **HM** | hesitation |
| **MM** | enjoyment |
| **BRR** | shivering |
| **CLY** | to steal |
| **CWM** | steep-sided hollow |
| **GYP** | to cheat |
| **HMM** | more hesitation |
| **HYP** | hypotenuse |
| **LYM** | leash |
| **MYC** | gene causing tumours |
| **PHT** | irritation |
| **RHY** | rye |
| **SWY** | Australian gambling game |
| **SYN** | since |
| **TWP** | stupid |
| **TYG** | mug with two handles |
| **VLY** | low marshy ground |
| **WYN** | Germanic character equivalent to W |

# 100 It's Even Colder Outside

4- and 5-letter words to alleviate a consonant crisis:

| | | | |
|---|---|---|---|
| **BRRR** | more shivering | **SKYF** | to smoke a cigarette |
| **BYRL** | to remove lumps in cloth | **SKYR** | Scandinavian cheese |
| **FYRD** | Anglo-Saxon militia | **SYPH** | syphilis |
| **GYMP** | to limp | **TRYP** | parasite |
| **GYNY** | gynaecology | **TYMP** | blast furnace outlet |
| **HWYL** | emotional fervour | **TYPP** | unit of thickness of yarn |
| **KYND** | kind | | |
| **LYCH** | dead body | **TYPY** | typifying breed of animal |
| **PFFT** | sudden disappearance | | |
| **RYND** | crossbar part of millstone | **WYCH** | tree |
| | | **WYND** | narrow lane |
| **SCRY** | to divine by crystal gazing | **XYST** | long portico |
| **SKRY** | to try to tell future | **YMPT** | repaired birds' wings |

Watch out for **CRWTH**, an ancient stringed Celtic instrument, and **CWTCH** – to be snuggled up. There's also the unlikely **PHPHT**, which expresses irritation.

**101** **The Endgame**

Making the most of the **endgame** is worthy of a book in itself. A few principles to follow once the bag is empty are:

(a) Assuming you can't use all your letters in one go, try to find a way of playing out in two turns, to give yourself the best chance of playing the last move of the game.

(b) Score as many points as possible over the two turns, ideally at the same time stopping your opponent from getting their best score or from playing out (you'll know their letters and what they can potentially play if you've tile tracked correctly).

(c) Think hard about which order to play the two turns in – it's often best to save the best to last and take the lower scoring move first, particularly if it stymies your opponent.

(d) If possible, set up a big scoring final move with your penultimate turn, especially if your opponent can't block it – even if they can, they may have to sacrifice vital points to do so.

(e) Bear in mind your **penultimate move** is really the most important of the whole game since it's the only one in which you can decide your next turn as well.

(f) In close games, the **endgame** is all-important. It's amazing how many wins you can eke out from a seemingly forlorn position – never give up.

## 102 | Four Nights in Bangkok

If you're getting eager and fancy trying out an international (English-speaking) Scrabble tournament, I would highly recommend the 'King's Cup' in Bangkok – effectively Thailand's national championship. Held every June, this is an incredible event, open to everyone. It takes place in the National Stadium, which is the only place big enough to accommodate the ever-increasing number of participants (it's getting close to 10,000).

There is an opening ceremony which features dancing girls and players welcomed on stage with their national flags. Then there's some pretty intense Scrabble for four days while the atmosphere positively buzzes, culminating in the finalists being serenaded to the sound of Queen's *We are the Champions*.

The winner gets a cheque for $10,000 from a member of Thailand's royal family and, if they are sensible, goes for a well-earned rest on one of Thailand's fantastic islands for a couple of weeks.

There's a host of other events on the international calendar – to find out more, take a look at the World English-language Scrabble Players' Association (WESPA) website – **www.wespa.org**

## 103 Over.....

You can get too much of a good thing with some of these:

OVERABLE

OVERBIG

OVERCOY

OVERDUST

OVEREGG

OVERFISH

OVERGILD

OVERHOLY

OVERIDLE

OVERJUST

OVERKNEE

OVERLEWD

OVERMILK

OVERNET

OVERPLUS

OVERRUDE

OVERSUDS

OVERTART

OVERURGE

OVERVEIL

OVERWILY

OVERYEAR

OVERZEAL

# 104 And Out

Here are some more out-standing words:

| | |
|---|---|
| **OUTADDS** | **OUTMARCH** |
| **OUTBITCH** | **OUTNAME** |
| **OUTCHEAT** | **OUTPITY** |
| **OUTDREAM** | **OUTQUOTE** |
| **OUTECHO** | **OUTRING** |
| **OUTFLASH** | **OUTSIZE** |
| **OUTGNAW** | **OUTTHROB** |
| **OUTHOWL** | **OUTVENOM** |
| **OUTJINX** | **OUTWHIRL** |
| **OUTKISS** | **OUTYELL** |
| **OUTLOVE** | |

# And So to Zed

There are some lovely 3-letter words involving the **Z**:

| | |
|---|---|
| **ADZ** | adze |
| **BEZ** | part of deer's horn |
| **BIZ** | business |
| **CAZ** | casual |
| **COZ** | cousin |
| **CUZ** | cousin |
| **FIZ** | fizz |
| **JIZ** | wig |
| **LEZ** | lesbian (*slang*) |
| **LUZ** | indestructible human bone |
| **MIZ** | misery |
| **MOZ** | jinx |
| **POZ** | positive |
| **RIZ** | past form of rise |
| **SAZ** | Middle Eastern instrument |
| **SEZ** | says |
| **TIZ** | state of confusion |
| **WIZ** | wizard |
| **ZAG** | to change direction sharply |
| **ZAX** | saxophone |
| **ZEA** | corn silk |
| **ZEE** | the letter Z |
| **ZEK** | Soviet prisoner |
| **ZEP** | long sandwich |
| **ZEX** | cutting tool |
| **ZIG** | to change direction sharply |
| **ZIN** | zinfandel |
| **ZIT** | pimple |
| **ZOA** | independent animal bodies |
| **ZOL** | cannabis cigarette |

Keep looking to play the **Z** across and down simultaneously on the premium squares – double gets you forty points, triple scores a hefty sixty.

# Worth a Read and a Watch

*Word Freak – Heartbreak, Triumph, Genius and Obsession in the World of Competitive Scrabble Players* is a best-selling book by Wall Street journalist Stefan Fatsis. It tells of an ordinary guy starting out in the 'Scrabble World' and is a really excellent read – the film rights have been bought by Curtis Hanson – director of *LA Confidential*.

*Word Wars – Tiles and Tribulations on the Scrabble Game Circuit* is a funny real-life documentary by Eric Chaikin, focusing on four top US Scrabblers.

*Collins Official Scrabble Words* (2015 edition) contains the full list of words allowed in Scrabble, without meanings, while *Collins Scrabble Dictionary* includes brief definitions for words from two to nine letters in length.

If you prefer full definitions, there's always *Collins English Dictionary* to while away the time.

For a bit of variety, Bananagrams®, Boggle, Channel 4's Countdown and Scrabble Trickster are all good Scrabble practice.

Facebook Scrabble is all the rage these days – you can have as many simultaneous games as you like. It's very sociable and highly addictive.

# Taking It Further

There are over 300 Scrabble clubs in the UK, normally meeting weekly with an average membership of fifteen. Two or three games are played over an evening in a variety of venues ranging from homes to pubs to village halls, and there are competitions, leagues and trophies to be won over a season.

Joining a club is the first step towards Scrabble seriousness and can be quite daunting to start with. Just remember the vast majority of club players are extremely pleasant and don't be put off by the overcompetitive minority.

There is a Scrabble event to be found somewhere in the UK on almost every weekend of the year.

The numbers of players can range from ten to a hundred, and the larger tournaments contain more than one division, so you're placed with players of a similar standard. There are usually six or seven games in a one-day event – weekends can take in around sixteen.

If you don't take it too seriously they can be great fun. The only big difference from playing at home or at a club is the use of timers to ensure the games last under an hour and no one holds up the schedule – they don't take long to get used to operating.

The ABSP is the Association of British Scrabble Players and is effectively the game's governing body.

It costs £15 a year to join (there are about 800 members), and for that you get an excellent bi-monthly newsletter and various tournament discounts. The ABSP website can be found at **www.absp.org.uk** and contains everything you need to know about what's going on in the 'Scrabble World'. There's a tournament calendar, event results, rankings and wordlists and plenty of other useful material for the aspiring player.

If you are interested in joining a Scrabble club, you can get all the information you need by visiting **www.absp.org.uk/play**

## The 124 two-letter words playable in Scrabble are...

| | | | | |
|-----|-----|-----|-----|-----|
| AA | DO | IF | NY | SO |
| AB | EA | IN | OB | ST |
| AD | ED | IO | OD | TA |
| AE | EE | IS | OE | TE |
| AG | EF | IT | OF | TI |
| AH | EH | JA | OH | TO |
| AI | EL | JO | OI | UG |
| AL | EM | KA | OM | UH |
| AM | EN | KI | ON | UM |
| AN | ER | KO | OO | UN |
| AR | ES | KY | OP | UP |
| AS | ET | LA | OR | UR |
| AT | EX | LI | OS | US |
| AW | FA | LO | OU | UT |
| AX | FE | MA | OW | WE |
| AY | FY | ME | OX | WO |
| BA | GI | MI | OY | XI |
| BE | GO | MM | PA | XU |
| BI | GU | MO | PE | YA |
| BO | HA | MU | PI | YE |
| BY | HE | MY | PO | YO |
| CH | HI | NA | QI | YU |
| DA | HM | NE | RE | ZA |
| DE | HO | NO | SH | ZO |
| DI | ID | NU | SI | |

## The 1341 three-letter words playable in Scrabble are...

| | | | | | |
|---|---|---|---|---|---|
| AAH | AID | AND | ATE | BAL | BOA |
| AAL | AIL | ANE | ATS | BAM | BOB |
| AAS | AIM | ANI | ATT | BAN | BOD |
| ABA | AIN | ANN | AUA | BAP | BOG |
| ABB | AIR | ANS | AUE | BAR | BOH |
| ABO | AIS | ANT | AUF | BAS | BOI |
| ABS | AIT | ANY | AUK | BAT | BOK |
| ABY | AJI | APE | AVA | BAY | BON |
| ACE | AKA | APO | AVE | BED | BOO |
| ACH | AKE | APP | AVO | BEE | BOP |
| ACT | ALA | APT | AWA | BEG | BOR |
| ADD | ALB | ARB | AWE | BEL | BOS |
| ADO | ALE | ARC | AWK | BEN | BOT |
| ADS | ALF | ARD | AWL | BES | BOW |
| ADZ | ALL | ARE | AWN | BET | BOX |
| AFF | ALP | ARF | AXE | BEY | BOY |
| AFT | ALS | ARK | AYE | BEZ | BRA |
| AGA | ALT | ARM | AYS | BIB | BRO |
| AGE | ALU | ARS | AYU | BID | BRR |
| AGO | AMA | ART | AZO | BIG | BRU |
| AGS | AME | ARY | BAA | BIN | BUB |
| AHA | AMI | ASH | BAC | BIO | BUD |
| AHI | AMP | ASK | BAD | BIS | BUG |
| AHS | AMU | ASP | BAG | BIT | BUM |
| AIA | ANA | ASS | BAH | BIZ | BUN |

| BUR | CIT | DAE | DIN | DUI | EIK |
|-----|-----|-----|-----|-----|-----|
| BUS | CLY | DAG | DIP | DUM | EKE |
| BUT | COB | DAH | DIS | DUN | ELD |
| BUY | COD | DAK | DIT | DUO | ELF |
| BYE | COG | DAL | DIV | DUP | ELK |
| BYS | COL | DAM | DOB | DUX | ELL |
| CAA | CON | DAN | DOC | DYE | ELM |
| CAB | COO | DAP | DOD | DZO | ELS |
| CAD | COP | DAS | DOE | EAN | ELT |
| CAF | COR | DAW | DOF | EAR | EME |
| CAG | COS | DAY | DOG | EAS | EMO |
| CAL | COT | DEB | DOH | EAT | EMS |
| CAM | COW | DEE | DOL | EAU | EMU |
| CAN | COX | DEF | DOM | EBB | END |
| CAP | COY | DEG | DON | ECH | ENE |
| CAR | COZ | DEI | DOO | ECO | ENG |
| CAT | CRU | DEL | DOP | ECU | ENS |
| CAW | CRY | DEN | DOR | EDH | EON |
| CAY | CUB | DEP | DOS | EDS | ERA |
| CAZ | CUD | DEV | DOT | EEK | ERE |
| CEE | CUE | DEW | DOW | EEL | ERF |
| CEL | CUM | DEX | DOY | EEN | ERG |
| CEP | CUP | DEY | DRY | EEW | ERK |
| CHA | CUR | DIB | DSO | EFF | ERM |
| CHE | CUT | DID | DUB | EFS | ERN |
| CHI | CUZ | DIE | DUD | EFT | ERR |
| CID | CWM | DIF | DUE | EGG | ERS |
| CIG | DAB | DIG | DUG | EGO | ESS |
| CIS | DAD | DIM | DUH | EHS | EST |

| | | | | | |
|---|---|---|---|---|---|
| ETA | FEN | FOX | GEM | GOX | HEH |
| ETH | FER | FOY | GEN | GOY | HEM |
| EUK | FES | FRA | GEO | GRR | HEN |
| EVE | FET | FRO | GER | GUB | HEP |
| EVO | FEU | FRY | GET | GUE | HER |
| EWE | FEW | FUB | GEY | GUL | HES |
| EWK | FEY | FUD | GHI | GUM | HET |
| EWT | FEZ | FUG | GIB | GUN | HEW |
| EXO | FIB | FUM | GID | GUP | HEX |
| EYE | FID | FUN | GIE | GUR | HEY |
| FAA | FIE | FUR | GIF | GUS | HIC |
| FAB | FIG | GAB | GIG | GUT | HID |
| FAD | FIL | GAD | GIN | GUV | HIE |
| FAE | FIN | GAE | GIO | GUY | HIM |
| FAG | FIR | GAG | GIP | GYM | HIN |
| FAH | FIT | GAK | GIS | GYP | HIP |
| FAN | FIX | GAL | GIT | HAD | HIS |
| FAP | FIZ | GAM | GJU | HAE | HIT |
| FAR | FLU | GAN | GNU | HAG | HMM |
| FAS | FLY | GAP | GOA | HAH | HOA |
| FAT | FOB | GAR | GOB | HAJ | HOB |
| FAW | FOE | GAS | GOD | HAM | HOC |
| FAX | FOG | GAT | GOE | HAN | HOD |
| FAY | FOH | GAU | GON | HAO | HOE |
| FED | FON | GAW | GOO | HAP | HOG |
| FEE | FOO | GAY | GOR | HAS | HOH |
| FEG | FOP | GED | GOS | HAT | HOI |
| FEH | FOR | GEE | GOT | HAW | HOM |
| FEM | FOU | GEL | GOV | HAY | HON |

| | | | | | |
|---|---|---|---|---|---|
| HOO | IMP | JIB | KED | LAD | LIE |
| HOP | ING | JIG | KEF | LAG | LIG |
| HOS | INK | JIN | KEG | LAH | LIN |
| HOT | INN | JIZ | KEN | LAM | LIP |
| HOW | INS | JOB | KEP | LAP | LIS |
| HOX | ION | JOE | KET | LAR | LIT |
| HOY | IOS | JOG | KEX | LAS | LOB |
| HUB | IRE | JOL | KEY | LAT | LOD |
| HUE | IRK | JOR | KHI | LAV | LOG |
| HUG | ISH | JOT | KID | LAW | LOO |
| HUH | ISM | JOW | KIF | LAX | LOP |
| HUI | ISO | JOY | KIN | LAY | LOR |
| HUM | ITA | JUD | KIP | LEA | LOS |
| HUN | ITS | JUG | KIR | LED | LOT |
| HUP | IVY | JUN | KIS | LEE | LOU |
| HUT | IWI | JUS | KIT | LEG | LOW |
| HYE | JAB | JUT | KOA | LEI | LOX |
| HYP | JAG | KAB | KOB | LEK | LOY |
| ICE | JAI | KAE | KOI | LEP | LUD |
| ICH | JAK | KAF | KON | LES | LUG |
| ICK | JAM | KAI | KOP | LET | LUM |
| ICY | JAP | KAK | KOR | LEU | LUN |
| IDE | JAR | KAM | KOS | LEV | LUR |
| IDS | JAW | KAS | KOW | LEW | LUV |
| IFF | JAY | KAT | KUE | LEX | LUX |
| IFS | JEE | KAW | KYE | LEY | LUZ |
| IGG | JET | KAY | KYU | LEZ | LYE |
| ILK | JEU | KEA | LAB | LIB | LYM |
| ILL | JEW | KEB | LAC | LID | MAA |

| | | | | | |
|------|------|------|------|------|------|
| MAC | MID | MUD | NIB | NYE | OLD |
| MAD | MIG | MUG | NID | NYM | OLE |
| MAE | MIL | MUM | NIE | NYS | OLM |
| MAG | MIM | MUN | NIL | OAF | OMA |
| MAK | MIR | MUS | NIM | OAK | OMS |
| MAL | MIS | MUT | NIP | OAR | ONE |
| MAM | MIX | MUX | NIS | OAT | ONO |
| MAN | MIZ | MYC | NIT | OBA | ONS |
| MAP | MMM | NAB | NIX | OBE | ONY |
| MAR | MNA | NAE | NOB | OBI | OOF |
| MAS | MOA | NAG | NOD | OBO | OOH |
| MAT | MOB | NAH | NOG | OBS | OOM |
| MAW | MOC | NAM | NOH | OCA | OON |
| MAX | MOD | NAN | NOM | OCH | OOP |
| MAY | MOE | NAP | NON | ODA | OOR |
| MED | MOG | NAS | NOO | ODD | OOS |
| MEE | MOI | NAT | NOR | ODE | OOT |
| MEG | MOL | NAV | NOS | ODS | OPA |
| MEH | MOM | NAW | NOT | OES | OPE |
| MEL | MON | NAY | NOW | OFF | OPS |
| MEM | MOO | NEB | NOX | OFT | OPT |
| MEN | MOP | NED | NOY | OHM | ORA |
| MES | MOR | NEE | NTH | OHO | ORB |
| MET | MOS | NEF | NUB | OHS | ORC |
| MEU | MOT | NEG | NUG | OIK | ORD |
| MEW | MOU | NEK | NUN | OIL | ORE |
| MHO | MOW | NEP | NUR | OIS | ORF |
| MIB | MOY | NET | NUS | OKA | ORG |
| MIC | MOZ | NEW | NUT | OKE | ORS |

| | | | | | |
|---|---|---|---|---|---|
| ORT | PAW | PIX | PUS | REF | ROE |
| OSE | PAX | PLU | PUT | REG | ROK |
| OUD | PAY | PLY | PUY | REH | ROM |
| OUK | PEA | POA | PWN | REI | ROO |
| OUP | PEC | POD | PYA | REM | ROT |
| OUR | PED | POH | PYE | REN | ROW |
| OUS | PEE | POI | PYX | REO | RUB |
| OUT | PEG | POL | QAT | REP | RUC |
| OVA | PEH | POM | QIN | RES | RUD |
| OWE | PEL | POO | QIS | RET | RUE |
| OWL | PEN | POP | QUA | REV | RUG |
| OWN | PEP | POS | RAD | REW | RUM |
| OWT | PER | POT | RAG | REX | RUN |
| OXO | PES | POW | RAH | REZ | RUT |
| OXY | PET | POX | RAI | RHO | RYA |
| OYE | PEW | POZ | RAJ | RHY | RYE |
| OYS | PHI | PRE | RAM | RIA | RYU |
| PAC | PHO | PRO | RAN | RIB | SAB |
| PAD | PHT | PRY | RAP | RID | SAC |
| PAH | PIA | PSI | RAS | RIF | SAD |
| PAK | PIC | PST | RAT | RIG | SAE |
| PAL | PIE | PUB | RAV | RIM | SAG |
| PAM | PIG | PUD | RAW | RIN | SAI |
| PAN | PIN | PUG | RAX | RIP | SAL |
| PAP | PIP | PUH | RAY | RIT | SAM |
| PAR | PIR | PUL | REB | RIZ | SAN |
| PAS | PIS | PUN | REC | ROB | SAP |
| PAT | PIT | PUP | RED | ROC | SAR |
| PAV | PIU | PUR | REE | ROD | SAT |

| SAU | SIG | SOX | TAM | TIE | TUP |
|-----|-----|-----|-----|-----|-----|
| SAV | SIK | SOY | TAN | TIG | TUT |
| SAW | SIM | SOZ | TAO | TIK | TUX |
| SAX | SIN | SPA | TAP | TIL | TWA |
| SAY | SIP | SPY | TAR | TIN | TWO |
| SAZ | SIR | SRI | TAS | TIP | TWP |
| SEA | SIS | STY | TAT | TIS | TYE |
| SEC | SIT | SUB | TAU | TIT | TYG |
| SED | SIX | SUD | TAV | TIX | UDO |
| SEE | SKA | SUE | TAW | TIZ | UDS |
| SEG | SKI | SUG | TAX | TOC | UEY |
| SEI | SKY | SUI | TAY | TOD | UFO |
| SEL | SLY | SUK | TEA | TOE | UGH |
| SEN | SMA | SUM | TEC | TOG | UGS |
| SER | SNY | SUN | TED | TOM | UKE |
| SET | SOB | SUP | TEE | TON | ULE |
| SEV | SOC | SUQ | TEF | TOO | ULU |
| SEW | SOD | SUR | TEG | TOP | UMM |
| SEX | SOG | SUS | TEL | TOR | UMP |
| SEY | SOH | SWY | TEN | TOT | UMS |
| SEZ | SOL | SYE | TES | TOW | UMU |
| SHA | SOM | SYN | TET | TOY | UNI |
| SHE | SON | TAB | TEW | TRY | UNS |
| SHH | SOP | TAD | TEX | TSK | UPO |
| SHO | SOS | TAE | THE | TUB | UPS |
| SHY | SOT | TAG | THO | TUG | URB |
| SIB | SOU | TAI | THY | TUI | URD |
| SIC | SOV | TAJ | TIC | TUM | URE |
| SIF | SOW | TAK | TID | TUN | URN |

| | | | | | |
|---|---|---|---|---|---|
| URP | VIM | WAY | WOS | YEN | ZAP |
| USE | VIN | WAZ | WOT | YEP | ZAS |
| UTA | VIS | WEB | WOW | YER | ZAX |
| UTE | VLY | WED | WOX | YES | ZEA |
| UTS | VOE | WEE | WRY | YET | ZED |
| UTU | VOG | WEM | WUD | YEW | ZEE |
| UVA | VOL | WEN | WUS | YEX | ZEK |
| VAC | VOM | WET | WUZ | YEZ | ZEL |
| VAE | VOR | WEX | WYE | YGO | ZEP |
| VAG | VOW | WEY | WYN | YID | ZEX |
| VAN | VOX | WHA | XED | YIN | ZHO |
| VAR | VUG | WHO | XIS | YIP | ZIG |
| VAS | VUM | WHY | YAD | YOB | ZIN |
| VAT | WAB | WIG | YAE | YOD | ZIP |
| VAU | WAD | WIN | YAG | YOK | ZIT |
| VAV | WAE | WIS | YAH | YOM | ZIZ |
| VAW | WAG | WIT | YAK | YON | ZOA |
| VEE | WAI | WIZ | YAM | YOU | ZOL |
| VEG | WAN | WOE | YAP | YOW | ZOO |
| VET | WAP | WOF | YAR | YUG | ZOS |
| VEX | WAR | WOG | YAS | YUK | ZUZ |
| VIA | WAS | WOK | YAW | YUM | ZZZ |
| VID | WAT | WON | YAY | YUP | |
| VIE | WAW | WOO | YEA | YUS | |
| VIG | WAX | WOP | YEH | ZAG | |